This Was Not on My Bucket List!

NAVIGATING "OLD SCHOOL" GRANDPARENTING IN A "NEWFANGLED" WORLD

BY LINDA MacCONNACHIE

ISBN: 978-1-7341262-9-7

Edited by: Dartinia Hull and Amy Ashby
Photos by: Darcy DeMart
Cover Illustration by: Katherine Messenger

Published by WARREN Publishing
Charlotte, NC
www.warrenpublishing.net
Printed in the United States

*With love to the sun and back, I dedicate this book to my
ten grandchildren, Ethan, Colin, Adelyn, Eliza, Kieran,
Conor, Teagan, Mary, Madison, and Padraig;*

AND

*To their parents, Megan and Michael;
Ian and Alison; Cameron and Kate,
who presented me with these precious gifts;*

AND

*To my husband, Ian (AKA PopPop),
Chief of the MacPac Clan*

"You Are My Sunshine."

Contents

The Beginning ...

I remember the day ... the day that changed my life forever.

My daughter and I had been to a three-day NAEYC (National Association for the Education of Young Children) conference out of town ... three-plus hours away ... same room ... same bed ... twenty-four hours a day *for three days*. I dropped her home and drove the last hour on to my house. Fifteen minutes later, she shows up at our front door. *Whaaat?* Before panic could set in, she quickly handed her dad a gift bag. SURPRISE! A cross-stitched Winnie the Pooh bib with "POP POP" in large print!

Stunned could best describe this situation. I mean, 300 miles, three days, and not a word? Needless to say, this was not at all on PopPop's radar, so he was slow to catch on. Not me! As soon as I saw that gift bag, my Nana genes kicked in to high gear and I mentally started knitting blankets.

Well, ten grandbabies later it is still a miracle each and every time a new life arrives—and each and every time I learn something new, because each and every one of these little bundles of joy is *so* different. Ever wonder how you could love the next one since your heart is already full? When our three children were little, as a new baby was coming along, we would light one candle together that represented Mommy and Daddy's love. Then we would light another candle from that flame for each child and ask if that Mommy-Daddy candle flame got smaller or brighter. The answer was always "brighter," because there were more flames, and there was more love. Our hearts have the amazing ability to grow. There is always enough LOVE—just not always enough laps to sit on, arms to hug away tears, and time for that Bucket List!

"FEW THINGS ARE MORE DELIGHTFUL THAN GRANDCHILDREN FIGHTING OVER YOUR LAP."
–DOUG LARSON

Introduction

Retirement was No. 1. The long-awaited day that spells **FREEDOM!** I had taught elementary school for a decade, owned two large child development centers for twenty-plus years, and sat on every board of directors I could find to advocate for children. So, after listening to skipping toddler feet, giggling preschoolers and, yes, crying babies, I was ready to "Hit the Road Jack"! I had helped raise thousands of children, counseled thousands of parents, and consoled thousands of grandparents and this was *my* time. I made a bucket list sixty-eight adventures long, and was set to go. Zipline over the rainforest in Costa Rica, fly an airplane, scuba dive, touch a tiger, and, for sure, yoga class three times a week. I planned on adding to this list as, in all probability, No. 40, which was a visit from Publishers Clearing House, was realistically never going to happen. I had imagined walking the shores of exotic beaches and viewing glorious sunsets hand-in-hand with my husband with the winnings, but we have since accepted that we'll have to learn how to travel on a budget.

Watching grandchildren was *not* on my bucket list. It never occurred to me. But we have been blessed with ten grandchildren. Wow! Ten grandchildren who live within thirty minutes. Double wow! I definitely won the Luckiest Nana in the World trophy! There are millions of baby boomers who would be green-eyed over just how lucky I am. I get to enjoy their laughter, their smiles, their enthusiasm, their energy, their curiosity, and their sleep-overs.

But being on speed dial meant life as we knew it was over. And we do deserve lives beyond being grandparents. We have raised our own children, and they are all feeding and clothing themselves. Been there, done that. Our generation worked long and hard at our chosen professions, counting the days until that retirement cake. Love those grands, but they can drain my energy bucket dry. So, when that SOS call comes in, sometimes we must JUST SAY NO! We can still be "The Greatest Grandparent in the World," but after a nap.

Love and guilt do not have to be incompatible emotions. It doesn't have to be about how many times we babysit, (well, I have never actually sat on a baby have you?) "child watch," or how many toys or clothes we buy them. It is the quality of time.

So, even if you are long-distance grandparents, you learn to Skype, Facetime, Zoom, video chat, or whatever you can to get that quality time that is important. Include your grands in what you are doing and encourage them to include you ... but only before 8 p.m.

Baby boomer grandparents come in all shapes, sizes, ages, races, religions, and cultures. One thing we all have in common is that we are officially allowed to spoil, love unconditionally, scoop ice cream with sprinkles before dinner, and *play*! My husband, AKA PopPop, officially earned his grandfather badge the day this business-suit-wearing guy was seen playing peek-a-boo in a restaurant.

But I must admit, sometimes, when the phone rings, we look at each other and say, "Who is out of school sick today?" "Who needs a ride to soccer?" "Whose child care is closed for a snow day?" "Spring Break?" I don't think this means we are going to Daytona Beach. The scramble begins to rearrange our own schedules, because, of course, our grands come first, "Forever and Ever, Amen." (Randy Travis said it best!)

I love watching my grands. But here's the hard part: How we were raised and how we raised our children is no way, anyway, comparable to any modern-day child rearing philosophy. As a new parent in the '70s with degrees in early childhood education and elementary education, I tended to modify conservative psychologist James Dobson's theory of setting boundaries and discipline, which was popular at the time, to meet our family needs.[1] Today, we encourage children to feel empowered, in control. We are encouraged to use reasoning and non-physical discipline. There seems to be a kinder, gentler philosophy. We are to be their friends. Truthfully, who is now ruling the roost?

Whether you are a Nana or a PopPop, a Meemaw or a PawPaw, a Grango or a Gramps, a Grandmamma or a Granddaddy, a Grannie or a Ga; whether you are an on-call, on-demand, speed-dial kind of grandparent; whether you are a long-distance Facetime grandparent; whether you are one of the three million grandparents raising your grandfamilies 24/7, I have walked in your shoes. I am a veteran at juggling those plates and this is my gift to you.

This wasn't on my Bucket List but ...

"HOW LUCKY I AM TO HAVE SOMETHING THAT MAKES SAYING GOOD-BYE SO HARD."
–WINNIE THE POOH

---

1   Dobson, James. *The New Dare to Discipline*. (Illinois: Tyndale Momentum, 1996).

CHAPTER 1

Just Bite Your Tongue, Zip Your Lips

I always imagined that by the time I was a grandparent, I would know all the answers. And I did. At least I thought I did! The problem was the rules of the game were changed by the time I got there. I realize every generation reinvents parenting, but seriously? Come on, people, children calling parents by their first name is not okay. Change usually creeps up on you, but this new drastically different parenting style has smacked me right upside the head. An editorial I read recently reminded me how things just aren't what they used to be. Here is a walk down memory lane and how things have changed.

- **Babies just happened.** Babies weren't planned around careers, finances, and social/

community service obligations. They weren't timed for the perfect moment. We all know there is no perfect moment. And there certainly were not reveal parties with pink or blue cupcakes.

- **Babies had real names.** Babies were probably named after a relative or a name the parents liked. In an effort to be unique and honor their culture, many parents are now being very creative in naming their newborns. Having been a child educator for so many years, our own daughter gave up on the Top 100 names as she was reminded of certain challenging children who came through her program. She selected girl name No. 843. PopPop claimed it was a made-up name for at least a year. No. 843 is now in the Top 100. Our Celtic/Scot grand names do create humorous roll-call experiences.
- **Birthday parties were in the backyard with your cousins.** We had one party where we threw marshmallows on a blanket and gave everyone a brown lunch bag with instructions to pick them up as fast as they could. Now, themed parties with castles built in the dining room and prince/princess thrones are more the norm. Pony rides, glow in the dark mini golf = money. Most schools have a rule you can't hand out invitations to just a few, the entire class must be invited. More money. I love how the schools

do allow families to paint the school spirit rock with birthday greetings for just a few dollars. My grands have had fun decorating the large rock with the birthday child's name, age, and soccer balls or unicorns to surprise their siblings.

- **Children rode bikes with no safety gear, and car safety meant you sat on someone's lap in the backseat.** Color-coordinated knee pads, helmets, and fancy-dancy car seats that snap into the stroller are a must today. Back in the day, I remember many head-over-handlebar spills when tears and sympathy were the cure-all. I also I remember my home economics teacher lecturing that if we ever, heaven forbid, had to sit on a boy's lap in the car, we were to have a newspaper between us. That rule is certainly a goner.

- **Children made friends in their neighborhood and at school.** Now there are scheduled play dates with the parents' friends' children's cousins ....

- **Parents didn't know what their children were up to every minute of the day.** In our more dangerous times and with the advent of helicopter parenting, many kids today are on shorter leashes. I must admit the first time my grandson drove three hours to the beach on a holiday weekend, I was the one watching my phone tracker. There really is an app for everything! As an early childhood educator who was responsible for the safety of so many children for so many years, I *still* watch. I can't help myself. On the other hand, I see many parents who condone unrestricted freedom and, honestly, it makes me a nervous wreck. PopPop had some grands at a park when a little girl came to sit with him on the bench. Her mom never took her eyes off her cellphone as her daughter talked to a stranger for thirty minutes. I *never* take my eyes off and have intervened on occasion for the safety of the child. One Walmart lockdown for a missing child and I am officially on-duty full-time. But children do need to experience independence and build self-confidence. Some situations warrant keeping a tight eye, but sometimes we have to let our kids learn on their own. We need to allow them the opportunity to grow away from us. Your goal should be to help balance your grand's desire for independence and decision making with their need for safety in today's world. With your confidence, love, and respect, this can be accomplished.

- **Children used to get verbal praise and a pat on the back.** For today's children, the parent's social media sites have become the trophy case of good deeds and awards, some well-deserved and some maybe not so much. Parents may not be as quick to praise in person, having said it all for the world to see. For those children and others without social media, a smiley face from the teacher may be as good as it gets. Unfortunately, for many of today's children, verbal praise and a pat on the back is not good enough. They think it is not worth doing if there is no reward in the end. WIIFM: what's in it for me?

- **Family time meant a trip to the park, a movie, or a meal at a restaurant.** For many, these same family time activities are still a priority. For *some*, however, it seems to be bigger and better and on a larger scale. Family time has expanded into extravagant vacation trips to exotic locations with some parents believing it is a necessity to "introduce children to other cultures." Or does it just look good on Facebook?

- **"Go out and play"** was practically the national anthem, and cuts and bruises were expected. Now if you can keep kids and teens off devices indoors or outdoors, it is a pleasant surprise.

- **Parents believed in spanking.** Those who were not spanked were considered spoiled. Today, one must *never* spank. Talking and correcting lovingly is the philosophy. BFFs. (Best Friends Forever).

- **Children showed respect for adults and authority figures (parents, police, and teachers).** As a former teacher and child care provider for over forty years, I have witnessed firsthand the significant decline in respect for all authority figures by many children and adults. When I was growing up, my parents and teachers taught me to respect authority. What the teacher said was a fact. What my parents said was the law. Parents today look in disbelief at the teacher when their child is disciplined and they make excuses for the behavior. There is no accountability, therefore, no respect. Of course, according to the parent, it is surely a lack of classroom management by the teacher. If parents don't show respect for the teachers, children won't. This must come from the home. Somehow that particular lesson has gotten lost in the shuffle. Lack of respect for parents is a natural progression when the adults in the household don't show respect for others or show leadership and command the respect of their own children. The same goes for the police. The majority of police officers are good, caring people trying to uphold the law. Those who get out, walk their beat, and know their neighborhoods are making a difference in the lives of the children in their district. They command respect. Let's encourage our children not to paint with such a broad brush that ALL parents, ALL teachers, ALL police officers are not to be respected or trusted. If an adult proves them wrong, time to reevaluate *that* person. Not *all* authority figures.

- **Children loved America.** I tear up every time Toby Keith sings, "And I'm proud to be an American, where at least I know I'm free … God bless the USA." Our country was founded as *one nation, under God*. The official motto of the United States is "In God We Trust." Tradition. Patriotism. This is what I believe in. Times have changed, however, and not everyone holds this same belief system. But that is what America is all about—*freedom*. Freedom to think your thoughts, speak your thoughts. However, I believe with prayer no longer in the school system or on the playing field, without the National Anthem being sung, without the flag being respected, our traditional patriotic values have diminished. I am working hard to instill this pride for our country in my grands. I am working hard to help my grands develop a moral citizenship with responsibility for personal conduct, public conduct, and civic leadership. Attending the Fourth of July parade and fireworks is not enough. We need to show them. We need to stand up and say, "I am proud to be an American" and honor the flag that still stands for our freedom.

- **Parenting advice came from friends, relatives, and teachers.** That is still true, but a couple of taps and the internet has experts available 24/7.

- **Bullying, temper tantrums, and ADHD were "kids being kids."** Today's parents are more informed about developmental problems that children face and more willing to take the effort to resolve these issues early. This is actually a good difference.

- **Toys were toys.** Now, toys are developmentally and age appropriate, gender neutral, multicultural, multigenerational, and exhibit differing abilities. Plus toys must be sparkly clean in our germophobic, "Don't put that in your mouth!" world. *Flashback:* Do you remember the joy of a cardboard box on Christmas morning, rather than the toy inside? Caution. Cardboard boxes can't be sanitized, so play with those at your own risk. Just kidding. Build that fort! Row that boat!

- **Bite your tongue, zip your lips.** You do not have to agree with, or embrace these changes, or agree with your children's decisions about family time and toy selection. You do have to bite your tongue and zip your lips about their parenting decisions, no matter how badly you think they need your advice. Unless they ask for it. If your mouth opens "by mistake," cover it with your hand and pretend to yawn. It is your job to worry about your grandchildren, but accept that your children's approach to raising their children may be different than yours. Parenting is really, really hard and many parents are unsure of what they are doing. The challenges they face in today's world are much greater than we experienced. Technology and social media have created warp speed situations we never had to deal with in real time. Do not nag; that will make them feel worse and even more insecure. Just like your grands, compliment your kids when you see good decisions being made. Support them in their decisions.

As much as you are tempted, resist the urge to "break the family rules." We do *bend* the family rules when our grands are at our house, but we must not undermine the parents. Find out which rules are non-negotiable, but suggest you be allowed to have some special rules of your own.

'Fess up. Have you broken a family rule and "forgotten" to mention it? We *all* have. Cap'n Crunch for dinner comes to mind for me! Get over the guilt. Grandparents are supposed to spoil. That is our purpose in life.

"IF YOU DON'T LIKE SOMETHING, CHANGE IT. IF YOU CAN'T CHANGE IT, CHANGE YOUR ATTITUDE."

–MAYA ANGELOU

CHAPTER 2

I'm Allergic to Broccoli!

"There are starving children in China!"
"Clean your plate or no dessert for you, young lady!"

How many times have we heard that threat from our parents? Did you ever hear those words coming out of your own mouth? We ate what was put in front of us and that was that. There were no negotiations in that take-it-or-leave-it kind of world where moms were not short order cooks.

Times have certainly changed since 1967, when 49 percent of women were stay-at-home moms who cooked a real meals with real food. Whether staying at home was by choice or by circumstance, it was a fact. Most moms were home. *Romper Room, Captain Kangaroo,* and *Mr. Rogers* kept children busy while mom was in the kitchen. There were very few boxed, frozen, or processed foods available for quick meals. Food was grown in family gardens and cooked without microwaves. Families ate together. Today, with the need for two incomes to provide any quality of life for the family, and with the availability of formal child care, as many as 75 percent of women work. The majority are full-time. This is our new reality. Frazzled parents dealing with a long work day, stressful commute, and picking up kids at three different child care facilities is *exhausting*. I get it. As parents were hauling car seats out of my centers, I often heard them say, "Gymnastics is in fifteen minutes. I have cereal in the car;" or "We have to get to soccer practice. Do you want McDonald's or Chick-fil-A?" (Fortunately, fast food restaurants have upgraded their healthy options for children). I get it.

The challenge is that our current over-scheduled culture fosters eating on the run and meals seem to be just an endless buffet that encourage children to become grazers. Stressed, overworked parents find it is much easier to allow the children to select what they might *really* eat (since when did macaroni and cheese become a new food group?) rather than making time to prepare a traditional, sit-down meal. This is detrimental to both good nutritional habits and family social time. Family mealtime together doesn't always have to be dinner.

Weekend breakfasts to kick off the Soccer Saturday marathon is a great Plan B.

So, when it is "Over the River and Through the Woods to Grandmother's House We Go" (like on Thanksgiving Day), convincing children that vegetables help them grow, or carrots are good for eyesight, may become a debatable discussion—and the drama begins. Sometimes this drama involves whining, crying, and stamping of feet. Hence, my granddaughter declaring, "I'm allergic to broccoli." This, by the way, is now one of her favorite foods. We must continue to fight the good fight. Remember, they are on your territory. You are the boss! Of course, then comes, "You are not the boss of me." Really? That is in a whole different chapter.

It is not our job to make every meal an adventure, but we certainly can make it special. Meals are a time for bonding, communication, manners, and healthy eating habits. For lucky days when we get those calls—"Can today be a sleepover day?"—we better have that refrigerator and pantry stocked with kid-friendly, parent-approved foods. Even better, when you have scheduled visits, prepare a taste-testing party on fancy plates and introduce some new and healthy foods. Make it fun! Chopped fresh fruit like kiwi, mango, papaya, and pears with some granola and vanilla yogurt on the side. Salsa and "white cheese" (queso blanco) are usually favorite dips so introduce cauliflower, snow peas, zucchini, cucumbers, or fresh green beans. Maybe a baked potato bar with cheese, bacon bits, peppers, onion, broccoli, and tomatoes? Work through the alphabet and see how many first letters they can find on their plates. Remember that 1970s Life cereal commercial on TV with three young brothers: "He likes it! Hey Mikey!"? Your grands will never know unless they try!

Back to parent-approved foods. When you are chief in charge of packing school lunches while parents are vacationing for a week, you better check before they leave about the rules and regulations. Without direction, I have caught my grands loading theirs lunch bags with chips, cookies, candy and soda cans. Oops! Do you remember saying to your own kids back in the day, "Get a brown bag, make a tuna fish or bologna sandwich on white bread. Grab a cookie and a lemonade?" The good news is today some of our younger generation have chosen a healthier lifestyle, actually shop at Whole Foods, and prefer kiddos to dine on almond butter, whole grain bread, and kale chips with an organic smoothie. Packed in a reusable container. Dishwasher safe!

When you feed children dinner, remember the standard USDA Food Pyramid: include a fruit, a vegetable, dairy, protein, and grains. This pyramid has actually been replaced by a Food Plate, which illustrates portions, but the basics are the same.

Look it up online. Encourage them to drink milk, juice, or water. I am not a fan of soda for many reasons, but if you have the energy to keep up with your grands or get them to sleep after a can of soda, that is on you! Fortunately, my grands call themselves "milk monsters," but going through four gallons of milk a week can be a financial challenge for young families.

- **Involve grands in food-decision time** and have them help you choose and prepare snacks and meals. They will be more likely to eat what is served. Limitless choices are your downfall. Giving them a "this or that" will eliminate many battles.

    Remember, without proper snacks, kids will be out of sorts and feeling moody, hyper, or tired. Just hand over a bag of powdered donuts and watch their world spin! But, when I hear "pretty please with a cherry on top!" as a grandparent, I figure that gives special dispensation, and they *can* have access to that glass jar of jelly beans that sits on top of the refrigerator. I know you must have a special candy bowl passed down from generation-to-generation, ready for when the grands visit. On my watch they can also have those ice cream sandwiches in the freezer. My mom did it; I'm doin' it! If you ask my three children, they will all say ice cream sandwiches at Grannie's house was a special childhood memory. Sometimes breaking the rules is worth the memory.

- **Model good choices** by picking healthy foods for you to eat. Fresh is best, but frozen is always better than canned. The food additives, dyes, and preservatives for a three- to five-year shelf life in canned goods often lead to health problems. (Really, do you expect a run on canned green beans three years from now, and you need to stock up?) Plus, the FDA has not followed other countries in banning common food dyes: Yellow 5 & 6; Red 3 & 40; Blue 1 & 2; and Green 3. These have been shown to lead to allergies and behavior issues. My advice is to become a label reader!

  One bad experience with red dye No. 40 and I learned *my* lesson. When I was nervous I chewed gum. Lots of gum. Three dermatologists later I discovered the facial rash, swollen lips, and swollen tongue were not due to anxiety. It was the cinnamon-flavored chewing gum full of Red Dye No. 40 that I smacked all day long. At least now I know. Forewarned is forearmed.

- **Do not overload the plates.** Especially if your mantra is "let me see that happy plate." Encourage children to eat a balanced meal and portion size so they can live a long and healthy life. I am certain it is not a surprise to you that childhood obesity is a serious issue with an estimated one in three American children qualifying as "obese." Learn to trust them when they say their bellies are full, but expect them to be back in thirty minutes to say they are sooo hungry.

- **Try to stay on their schedule.** Especially infants! Our newest newbie had just started to sit in a high chair, but before his applesauce was even served, his head was on the tray, and he was snoring to beat the band. His seven-year-old big sister rubbed his little head softly saying, "Wake up. You can't fall asleep at the dinner table. Sir, sir, it is not appropriate to go to bed on the table."

Almost EVERY family has "The Picky Eater." Children turning up their noses at your perfectly balanced meal is an age-old tradition, and it is frustrating and worrisome to parents and grandparents. Be assured, all those kids who lived on plain ol' peanut butter and grape jelly on white bread with the crust cut off for fifteen years have survived! I will never forget when our No. 1 son who did survive on peanut butter, grape jelly, and white bread for fifteen years proclaimed at a restaurant that he now liked fish. As it turned out, it was really a hush puppy, but you take what you can get and count it as an addition to his picky palate.

Toddlers become pickier around two years old and so it begins. Don't be discouraged if you hear "NO!" or even worse, if the little guy blows a raspberry and those carrots end up all over your glasses.

When worry takes over that your grandchild will go to bed hungry, it is okay to go to Plan B and just say, "Go put the bagel in the toaster yourself." Pick your battles.

But keep on serving beans, broccoli, and meats and encourage your grands to taste a bite. They might not like it today, but maybe they will tomorrow. It is your responsibility to try. Try again. And again.

And keep saying, "You get what you get and you don't pitch a fit."

It may be wishful thinking, but with four children, my daughter has a sign over her kitchen table that I love:

DINNER CHOICES
1. TAKE IT
2. LEAVE IT

CHAPTER 3

From Wooden Spoons to the Negotiating Table

My first memory of the wooden spoon was when my ninety-five-pound, five-foot mom was driving my two brothers and me from Florida to her family tobacco farm in North Carolina. We were not hooligans, but we knew she was focused on driving, so the back seat quickly became the Wild Wild West.

"He touched me!"

"She's looking at me!"

"He's on my side!"

Big, big, big mistake. Mom whipped out that long-handled wooden spoon, started swinging, and quickly there was a truce that lasted at least 100 miles. I'm not certain she made contact, but the threat was there. Things changed for the worse for us, though, once we got to the tobacco farm. Our grandmamma and granddaddy's Discipline 101 philosophy was the hickory stick. We even had to go snap the branch ourselves. Having raised nine children, believe me, Grandmamma was an expert and had no qualms about using that stick. I still hear those words, "Get yourself behind the woodshed."

I figured the wooden spoon worked well enough for my mom, so that was my first line of defense with my own young'uns. My children are quick to remind me of how that theory failed big time. I remember chasing all three around the dining room table and never catching them. If only I'd had a woodshed …. But for my husband, the tradition of "the heavy hand" was more successful, and those stories have been passed down to the grands. I can remember when No. 2 son was about three, hands on hips, he said he would have to use the heavy hand on his imaginary monkey after it had run out into the road. (Sorry, No. 2, "real monkey.") I am quite sure his children will find humor in this when they're grown, that is, after they are done experiencing the "heavy hand."

Then there was the dreaded principal's paddle. As an elementary school teacher, corporal punishment was not an option for me in the '70s, but the power of just being sent to the principal's office had my own children shaking in their boots. When visiting a local history museum recently, there was a mid-

1900s principal's paddle from our county elementary school displayed. The culprits' names had been inscribed, and I was shocked, just shocked to see how many of our community movers and shakers were listed on that paddle. The saying, "Spare the rod, spoil the child" was verified.

Fast forward to the twenty-first century. We are in a time when parents want to be "friends" with their children, which has created a whole generation of mini-CEOs at the negotiating table who can take down even the best of us. With the many parenting styles today, it is no wonder children, parents, and grandparents are confused. Back in the day, we just watched *Father Knows Best*, read Dr. Spock, and that was that.

Let's talk about the new parenting styles:

- **Authoritative** parenting style is widely-regarded as the most effective and beneficial. These parents have high expectations of their children, but also give positive feedback and nurturance. The child's day has structure, with household rules and planned bedtimes. There are consequences. There is communication. This type of parenting creates the healthiest environment.

- **Authoritarian parents** are the "do as I say," tough love, "my way or the highway" style. Mistakes may be punished harshly. Parents are demanding and strict. Punishment is the solution to all problems. The over-doers are the scary ones. You know who I am talking about. They are the parents who show up in court for abuse and neglect, and are the same ones you see on the front page of the newspaper. The children in these environments tend to have low self-esteem, become hostile, and show anger.

- **Permissive, free-wheeling, BFF parents** are indulgent, too soft, and lax in setting limits. You have seen these people in Target, with children running through the aisles and pulling items off of the shelves. I had one little dude in my center I caught walking barefoot down the hallway, stepping on every single drying finger-paint masterpiece. His mother was right beside him. I questioned Mom. "He's having a sensory experience," she said. Well, what about the eighteen other children who just lost *their* sensory experience? Permissive parents rarely enforce rules and offer few consequences. They think their child learns best with little interference. "Kids will be kids." These children are more likely to struggle academically and exhibit behavior issues. They don't respond to authority figures or rules. They are also at a higher risk for health problems such as obesity and dental issues, because parents don't enforce good habits. They tend to grow up with little self-discipline.

- **Uninvolved parents** just don't care. One of my worst days at my center was witnessing a mom's response to a three-year-old proudly showing her artwork of the day. I was shocked when the mom said, "I can't even tell what this is," crumpled it up, and threw it in the trash right there in the lobby. I don't know whose tears were bigger—mine or the child's. I couldn't help it. The words, "Oh, no! She worked so hard on that" just came out of my mouth. I actually went to the trash, got the artwork, straightened it out, and handed it back to the child. All under the evil eye of Mom. These parents don't ask about school or homework. They rarely know where the children are or who they are with. They certainly don't spend time with them. They expect the children to raise themselves. This is the most harmful style of parenting. In fairness, not all uninvolved parents are intentionally so. There could be mental health or substance abuse issues. This is when so many grandparents step in, step up. There are over three million grandparents raising their grandchildren 24/7, many because of termination of parental rights, or because their children are in jail or just MIA. Here these folks thought their years of raising children were over ....
- **Helicopter parents** over-help, step in, and over-do for the child. Hover. We all had to make

that volcano for our science fair project in elementary school, and probably received help from an adult, but no way does an eight-year-old even come up with the idea of measuring the PH content of common acidic beverages and examining how it corrodes metal. Plus, the child's project board looks like a graphic designer tediously created this work of perfection. Helicopter parents are overprotective and take an excessive interest in their children. These children have a harder time learning to manage their own emotions and behavior due to their parents having solved most of their problems. Decision making becomes difficult for the child. They are deprived of the need to self-motivate so the "get up and go" needed in real life might not be there. Great employee potential right?

Which parenting style sounds like YOU? But more importantly, which one is most like your own children? Understanding and recognizing your child's parenting style will make it much easier for you to manage their children. It is important to respect their guidelines and rules. In reality, most of us are a combination of all five of these parenting styles to some degree, depending on the day, the situation, and the child, and that is okay. I am the Helicopter Queen. I just can't help myself.

Time to discipline: What DO you do? What CAN you do?

- Take a deep breath or three. You know how the flight attendant says, "Put on your own mask first"? You need to get yourself together and download calm. DO NOT SAY, "Wait until your parents get home." Focus on the problem, not the child. You can handle this.

- Avoid unrealistic threats like, "If you throw that one more time, you will never watch TV again!" or "You better stop crying or I will give you something to cry about." One of my favorites, actually. Oh well.

- If you choose to negotiate, make it short and sweet. "It's okay to be upset;" "It's okay to feel how you feel. But it is not okay to … (hurt your friend);" "Let's have a do-over." Hear them out. Give two choices. You can do this … or this … end of discussion. The more you continue to talk, the more opportunities your grand has to work their magic.

- Walk away. Ignoring your grand can be very powerful. Children want and need your attention, good or bad. When the whining begins, look the other, or pretend you can't hear. Pay attention only when they finally realize they have to show positive behavior for you to respond.

- Time-out is not a personal favorite, as I prefer redirection to a quiet, safe place to let my grands get themselves together. But if a "thinking chair" in the corner works for you, keep in mind *one minute per age of the child,* with a maximum of five minutes. You will accomplish nothing if you expect your grand to sit fifteen to thirty minutes. *Dennis the Menace* is the exception, not the rule.

- Take away favorite things or activities. This can be more painful than a quick spanking. Twenty-four hours is long enough to learn a lesson for little ones. However, your grand should have to earn back the favorite thing or activity. Depending upon the situation, earning back could be shorter than twenty-four hours. Word of advice: never withhold meals. Treats, yes. Meals, no.

- Help your grands to learn the world does not always go their way and to seek solutions. Ask, "What would have been a better way to handle this?"

Remember:
- Reward GOOD behavior.
- Praise GOOD behavior.
- Model GOOD behavior.
- Don't Take Things Personally

"WHEN LITTLE PEOPLE ARE OVERWHELMED
BY BIG EMOTIONS, IT'S OUR JOB TO
SHARE OUR CALM, NOT THEIR CHAOS."

–L.R. KNOST

CHAPTER 4

Because I Said So!

TANTRUMS, MELTDOWNS, DEFIANCE, AND BITING

Tantrum is defined as an uncontrolled outburst of anger and frustration, typically in a young child. Synonyms: fit of rage, outburst, blow-up, frenzy, huff, scene, hissy fit.

Hmmmm. No definition needed for me. When my grand is in the middle of an emotional tornado, it is hard for me not to have my own meltdown, stomp my own foot, and yell, "because I said so!" The most memorable tantrum for me was a flailing four-year-old on the floor of Kmart right next to that day's "Blue Light Special." I am not sure which caused the customers to come running faster! I can tell you that Kmart sold a lot of non-stick pans that day.

Young children have not developed the coping or communication skills needed to convey their wants, needs, and frustrations. When you don't respond to what they are "saying," then their only recourse is *a meltdown*. Tantrum on!

The best thing you can do, if your grand is not endangering herself or others, is to take a breath, stay calm, and walk away. *Do not reinforce this negative behavior.* Take away your attention. This is when I kind of thought Kmart was going to call Child Protective Services, but it worked out okay that day. However, most public tantrums are better handled outside. Let the child know you know how they are feeling: frustrated, mad, sad. Offer the option of going to another room, or sitting in the car or on a bench to settle down. Giving your grand a choice gives back the feeling of some control to the child. Lack of control is probably what set the tantrum off in the first place. Public tantrums are stressful to everyone around, but how you react is what is most important. If you are calm, and look like you are in control, even if you are not doing anything, you will be perceived differently than if you are screaming threats and yanking the child by the arm. Remember how you have felt when you witnessed this type of adult behavior. Don't be that person.

Sometimes children just need to get the anger out so let them, but when the dust settles, and the tantrum is over, it is important to follow through with the original situation that caused the meltdown. No bribery allowed. If they won't pick up their toys, do not say, "I will give you a cookie if you do." You are reinforcing negative behavior. When they pick up the toys (and they eventually will), say, "Great job."

Defiance is defined as bold disobedience. "You are not the boss of me!" usually hits around six or seven years old. Even those sweet, well-adjusted children exhibit instances of strong-willed behavior and disrespectful speech. Around this time they also begin to discover their newfound independence. Add in the fact that all of a child's body cells are replaced by age seven, and there is a whole new little human you are dealing with.

Testing their boundaries and your patience is the norm. We used to call that getting too big for their britches. But did you ever say, "NO!" to an adult? The good old days of going along with what everyone else is doing is no longer a reason to do things. Reasoning with kids will not work. This is the time when boundaries, and limits need to be established and reinforced. Believe it or not, children really do want boundaries, which means you need to establish yourself as the "boss" of your house ASAP. Even our littlest ones know how to answer when asked, "what is Rule No. 1?" There is a quick chorus of "no running in the house." Keep rules simple, direct, and clear. We have ours numbered so we can just say, "What is rule No. __?"

There are many reasons a child will act out in defiance, however, they do need the opportunity to rectify their hurtfulness to others. Having them apologize at a very young age is of no value as they do not understand the concept. At six or seven, drawing an "I'm sorry" picture or writing a note gives them the time to think about their hurtful words or actions. "I'm sorry" without empathy = no lesson learned.

Lovingly remind the child you really are the "boss" and you expect their behavior to be better in the future.

Remember:
- Reinforce positive behavior. The more favorable attention they get for positive behavior, the more likely they are to do it again. Recognize positive behavior throughout the day, not just at tantrum time.
- Pay attention to what situations set your grands off, and be one step ahead. Keep healthy snacks in your purse for emergency tummy growling. Even (or should I say, "especially") teens can go into a funk without food every fifteen minutes. My oldest grand boy carried the nickname "Melty Boy" quite a while because he would crash without food.

Delayed nap times can cause rapid tailspins. Think of how cranky you get when the munchies set in or you stayed up too late for just one more episode of that TV show you have been binge-watching.

- Teaching sign language to infants and toddlers helps them to communicate past the fifty vocabulary words they may know, eliminating some frustrations. More, milk, juice, eat, cookie, tired, please, and thank you are all easily learned before the first birthday. Toddlers have the ability to learn twenty to forty or more signs. My personal favorite is, "I love you." I sign it while driving away or from across the elementary gymnasium during the Grandparents Day Celebration. When grands sign back, or better yet, sign "I love you" first, it melts my heart. Of course, we did have one grand boy who created his own sign. We never knew what it meant, but he used it only when he was around our "gang." Hence, we called it his "gang sign."

- Children have very short attention spans. Two to three minutes times age. If you feel a tantrum coming on, DIVERSION 101 calls for you to bring on your very best acting skills. Time to swing that Walmart buggy around to go look at the goldfish tanks. Be enthusiastic when you ask for the child's help to count the fish. There is a reason many dentists' offices have fish tanks. CALM ... ME ... DOWN!

- Help to settle your grand with a firm (not snuggly) hug. A deep hug can help the child to settle. Pressure on the palm also helps energies to center and the child feel calm and secure.
- Always make it about the behavior, not the child. You *don't* like the behavior. You *do* love the child.
- There is a time and place for good old fashion bribery. When you are heading to a recital, museum, restaurant, planetarium, etc. that you know will give your grand the squiggles and wiggles and/or hit some hot buttons, bribery is okay as long as it is on your terms *and* before the event.

Biting – No definition needed. Here is a scenario I am certain you can relate to. You have one grandtoddler on your lap and another snuggled up close, reading *Curious George* and suddenly there are screams, tears, and bedlam. The tear-streaked, snuggled up toddler is holding her arm, mumbling what to her says, "She bit me!" How in the world are you going to explain those bite marks to the parents? Especially if the skin is broken. Especially since the culprit was sitting on your own lap *and* it happened in a blink of an eye. Toddlers are *fast*.

Immediately give the bitten child more attention than the biter. Comfort her, kiss her boo-boo, wash with warm, soapy water, and put on a *Little*

Mermaid bandage. *Then* use your adult voice to tell the biter, "No biting! You have hurt your, sister [cousin, friend]." Never bite the child back, yell, or spank. Negative attention may encourage future biting. Remember, children don't care what kind of attention they get—good or bad—as long as they get attention. I like to have the biter actually put the bandage on the bitten child. They already associate bandages with their own boo-boos and this possibly will help them understand they hurt their sister, cousin, or friend.

What can trigger biting?
- Just being a toddler. Almost every toddler will try to bite or bite just because.
- Lack of language skills. Toddlers cannot say what they want to say, or ask for what they want. If they want that toy, biting is one way to get it.
- Overstimulation. Sometimes they just get so excited they lose control.
- Crowding. Toddlers do have a sense of personal space and sometimes they just don't want to share that space.
- Teething. Sometimes their mouth just hurts and biting soothes.

What can you do?

- Tell your grand that the next time they feel angry, they should ask you for help.
- Teach them to sign or say, "stop." This helps them to communicate. Use words, not teeth.
- Watch for signs of potential overstimulation. Redirect the child to a quiet place. This is not "time-out."
- If new teeth are on the horizon, cold wash cloths to chew on feel good, but are a little messy. A chilled teething ring works better, but a regular wash cloth will do. Snacks like a frozen mini-bagel to chew on work that lower mandible jaw as it is growing and shifting. There is now teething jewelery you can wear for your grand to chew on while they sit on your lap. There are over-the-counter solutions, but gone are the days of the Paregoric we rubbed on our own children's gums. Turns out that magical potion contained powdered opium. If we only knew … I wonder how many parents would have been tempted to use it themselves at three o'clock in the morning!
- Never bite your grand in play. I know it is hard to resist nibbling on those adorable fingers and toes, but it is definitely sending the wrong message. You don't want, "I'm going to eat your toes" to be literally translated!

- *Teeth Are Not for Biting* is a great board book by Elizabeth Verdick. Check it out.

One of my grand girls was a biter. It was her bad luck she attended my center. In a moment of frustration, I had told her if she bit again, I would put soap on her tongue. Soon I heard her coming down the hallway with her teacher, crying, "No soap, Nana!" That dab of soap was not one of my finer moments, but it worked! Biting is normal, but it is tough being a watchdog.

> "AT THE ROOT OF EVERY TANTRUM AND POWER STRUGGLE ARE UNMET NEEDS."
>
> –MARSHALL B. ROSENBERG

CHAPTER 5

Beyond Safety Pins and Duct Tape

Two of my most prominent childhood memories are that my grandmother kept about a thousand safety pins in her pocketbook, and my grandfather could produce a roll of duct tape faster than Spiderman shoots his spidey web. I always knew my grandparents were *ready* for any and all emergencies. Many hysterical tears were avoided with their quick action. Throw in a bobby pin or two and life was good.

Safety today has taken on a whole new meaning. Gone are the days when children played outside until the street lights came on. Today's parents are more like, "I'll drive you. Text me when you need a ride home." Gone are the days when there were only three television channels to select from and those shows were of heroes like *Davy Crockett*; dramatic stories like *Lassie*; and family values shown in *Leave It to Beaver*. Kids could walk to Woolworth's for an ice cream sundae or watch *American Bandstand* and *Soul Train* and hear lyrics they could understand with a beat they could dance to. Kids understood money was tight and saving S&H Green Stamps for a stereophonic record player or twenty-three-inch TV console became an activity the family did as a *family*.

In today's world, children are bombarded with color and noise and "busyness" all around them. They are constantly being entertained; their ears are plugged with ear buds and their eyes are on cellphones, texting. Today's children have become numb to their natural habitat and the dangers around them, leaving them vulnerable, at risk, and without the tools to survive. Don't worry. Helicopter parents will come to the rescue.

As grandparents, we need to recognize we can't fix today's world. We can pledge, however, to help keep our grandchildren stay safe.

- **Know their names. Know how many children are in your care.** I am NOT kidding. With ten grands, plus their moms, dads, grand dogs, and Nana and PopPop, one Christmas, as a joke, I received photo name tags for everyone to wear. Not so much a joke as I *really* needed those name tags. In our immediate family, plus grand dogs, we have a total of six names beginning with the "K" sound; four beginning with "E" sound; and four beginning with an "M" (not counting all those mommies). Only two "A" and one each for T, L, P.

One of our newbies named herself. No. 2 son had all boy names picked for the new arrival. When a little girl popped out, they just started calling out names for a family vote. She finally raised her tiny hand and it was another "M" name. Oh, well. It would be easier to number them as Dr. Seuss does in order of birth like Thing 1, Thing 2.

It is a good plan to also teach your grands your name. Your *real* name. You never know when they might need it. Have you heard over the intercom, "Will Jimmy's Nana please meet him at Customer Service?" Yikes! How many Jimmy Nanas are in the store? Keeping up with grandchildren is a whole different experience than shopping on your own. I decided early on that shopping with grands is definitely a bribe-worthy experience. No shame in it. One child in the pack is so easy to lose while you are deciding which brand oatmeal you might convince them to eat. My best advice: keep counting heads! Or else you are in for a game of *Where's Waldo?* in Walmart.

- **Know when to call the parents.** So, the parents are on their long-awaited, much-deserved second honeymoon, and you have been instructed not to call under any circumstances unless ...
  - Make certain those "unlesses" are determined in advance. Make sure they are extreme, need-to-know emergencies.
  - Make certain you have an itinerary of where and when parents will be changing locations. This includes requesting they keep phones charged and maybe even buying them an extra charger in case they try to sneak off the grid.
  - Make certain you have an emergency plan contact sheet (doctor, dentist, and neighbor) and specific instructions on when parents do want to be notified or when the neighbor could help (like if you cannot figure out the new math homework—ha!). If the parents come home and the police haven't been to the house, consider it a success.

    One of our own second honeymoons, we arrived home to a dead bird (funeral over), a broken dishwasher, *and* a police visit. That "do not call under any circumstances" rule really worked for us! Except, the police visit did put our young college girl sitter over the edge. Neighbors to the rescue!

Fortunately, the police were at the wrong house. That's just life in a college town.

- Make certain you have a current signed consent form for medical and/or emergency treatment. Remember, any new baby needs to be added to this form! You also need a copy of the family insurance card. Any trip to the ER or doctor will certainly require parent notification. But the doctors cannot help your grand if they do not have a written consent form in hand from the parents. Verbal over the phone consent doesn't count, and emailing it from another time zone takes precious time. All ten of my grands go to the same pediatrician and she knows me well. How great is that?

- Make certain you know where that epinephrine pen is and how to use it! You also have to be *prepared* to use it. Sticking our little people with needles is not what we wake up every morning hoping to do. Get over yourself. Practice! But thank goodness our six-year-old peanut-allergy grand has learned to handle this duty himself. After one school birthday party episode, he has also become a label reader. He has learned not to rely on the parent or teacher's word and checks for himself to see if the cupcake packaging says, "may contain peanuts" or "manufactured in a facility that processes tree nuts." Our other pen-carrying grand has a shellfish allergy that is airborne. Now *this* is a challenge. Cooking shrimp on a beach vacation is a requirement. Right? Antihistamines in advance work great; Benadryl to the rescue!

- **Know when to call 911.**
  - A child is choking.
  - A child has a broken bone.
  - A child is not responsive.
  - A child has a severe head injury.
  - A child ingests toxic chemicals: **POISON CONTROL 1-800-222-1222**.
  - A child receives a severe burn.
  - You feel the child's safety is in danger.

Follow the New Rules!

Parenting styles have changed since the good ol' days with Dr. Spock and so have the rules. Safety plugs in the wall sockets are not enough. Through research, many of our common practices are now considered life-threatening to today's children. (*What?* Our kids survived! WHEW!) I guess we just didn't know any better. Fortunately, our own children tend to make allowances for us as they really want our help. Actually, they need our help. As much as they need us, keeping our opinions to ourselves is a whole different matter. Just bite your tongue, zip your lip. The parents are the parents.

Car Seats

Remember how, as a child, you would call dibs on the deck behind that back seat as the primo place to ride? Or you'd ride in the back of a pickup truck with the wind blowing in your hair, and bugs hitting your face?

Excited by life, fresh out of law school, degree in hand, we splurged on a 1971 blue Corvette and what a dream car that was ... until baby No. 1 came along! Car seats weren't really "a thing" at that time. Apparently back in the day, the focus was not on protecting the child, but on looking cute. We thought that little yellow plastic baby seat with a harness was just fine, sitting at my feet in the passenger seat. We were off from the hospital, hitting eighty-five to ninety miles-per-hour! I cringe when I think of it now.

Child passenger laws were not passed until 1985, but have become stricter and ticketable offenses. One memorable family trip involved four straight hours of one grand girl talk ... talk ... talking. Finally falling asleep, the seat belt slipped off her shoulder, just in time for the state trooper to stop us for speeding, a state trooper who felt it her duty on this holiday weekend to inspect every inch of the van. This included the third row seat in the way,

way back. Apparently, even though our grand girl was buckled up, the shoulder strap was not in the correct position, so the trooper whipped out her seat belt violation ticket book, and we were off with ticket in hand. As far as we were all concerned, that seat belt violation ticket was money well spent just for the ten minutes of peace and quiet. And then the peace and quiet was over.

Today, the child's age, size, and developmental needs determine the correct car safety seat. The best investment you can make is a universal base and extra car seats for quick kid swaps. If you don't have an extra seat, just make certain the car seat itself gets belted in during the quick swap. Not *just* the child. I rue the day when, one right turn out of the driveway, my grand girl and her car seat flipped upside down in the back seat. She was belted in tightly and suspended between the seats. No tears from her—being the fourth child in an active household, this was just another adventure.

Many police stations, fire stations, hospitals, state police, and highway patrol offices will do free installation inspections. Just make certain they have a certified child passenger safety technician on site. Proper installation boosts safety, and hospitals will not release newborns unless you have a properly installed car seat. Most child care centers will have loaners for emergency pickups.

FYI—car seats do expire. If you currently are using the same infant seat you used for your now seventeen-year-old grandchild, you best go shopping! Most consignment stores no longer sell car seats because of the safety requirements. Use caution if buying second-hand from a friend or a garage sale. Check for recalls, cracks, and manufacture date label.

- **Infants and Toddlers:** All infants and toddlers are safer riding in a rear-facing seat until their height and weight allow them to face forward. Law requires rear-facing until after their first birthday. Rear facing is actually recommended until at least age two, or until the child exceeds the weight limit for rear facing according to the manufacturer's guidelines. Never place a rear-facing car seat in front of an active airbag.
- **Toddlers and Preschoolers:** Children who have outgrown their rear-facing car seat should ride in the back seat in a forward-facing car seat with harness as long as possible and/or up to the highest weight or height the manufacturer allows.
- **School-aged children:** All children who exceed the height and weight guidelines for their forward-facing safety seat should use a belt-positioning booster seat. This is typically when the child reaches four feet nine inches in height, is eight through twelve years of age, or when the seat belt fits properly on its own.

- **Older children:** Continue using a booster seat until a child is large enough or old enough for the vehicle seat belt to fit them. A properly-fitted shoulder belt crosses the middle of the shoulder (not the neck) and a properly fitted lap belt rests on the hips (not the stomach). All children under the age of thirteen should ride in the back seat. If the vehicle does not have a back seat and the child must ride in the front, the air bag must be disengaged.

I seem to have my very own car safety patrol captain. One day, I was driving and I heard this little voice coming from the back seat, "ten and two, Nana." Apparently my hands were not properly positioned on the steering wheel, but at least I had made certain that the grand was in the correct booster seat and it was attached properly to the back seat.

Cribs

Do you remember the excitement of shopping, shopping, shopping for the new baby's nursery? All the fluffy, snuggly blankies? Cute, matching bumper pads, curtains, and sheets? Stuffed bears, bunnies, and bumble bees?

As parents and grandparents, we have learned so much since 1994 when "Safe to Sleep" was initiated. This initiative encouraged parents to have their children sleep on their backs. SIDS (Sudden Infant Death Syndrome) is the leading cause of death for infants ages one through twelve months. Most crib deaths occur within the first two to four months, and 90 percent of SIDS cases occur at younger than six months of age. Scary, right? The SIDS rate is higher during winter because one of the stressors is increased body temperature. In the winter, we layer, bundle, and cover babies because *we* are cold. Just because they have cold hands and feet doesn't mean *they* are cold. Check their armpits to get a better idea of how hot or cold they really are. The good news is SIDS crib deaths have declined by 50 percent since this initiative was backed by the US National Institute of Child Health and Human Development.

So what can you do to reduce risk and promote the use of safe sleep practices?

- **Back to sleep!** Put concerns over a flat head or bald spots aside. No "in my day" talk. Alternate back sleeping with supervised awake "tummy time" one or more times a day. Tummy time builds strength, supports motor development, and prevents flat heads and bald spots.
- **NO fluffy, snuggly blankets. NO matching cute bumper pads. NO stuffed bears, bunnies, and bumble bees.** This "no cute things" rule reduces accidental suffocation or strangulation. Only a pacifier should be in the crib or sleep

place. Pacifiers are believed to be protective against SIDS.

- **Swaddling** is a practice of tightly wrapping an infant so that arms and legs are restricted for warmth and security. Just not too tight! Modern-day swaddlers with hook-and-loop fasteners are awesome. Swaddling helps infants to fall asleep and stay asleep, and helps them to stay on their backs. Some infants prefer arms out, and that can be easily accomplished with adjusting the swaddle blanket or sleep sack. Babies should only be swaddled until they are old enough to roll over onto their bellies.

- **Controlled room temperature** of sixty-eight to seventy-two degrees. Keep it cool! Do not over-dress or over-bundle. Remember that core body temperature mentioned earlier. Do not put a blanket over the infant. Swaddling helps regulate warmth.

- **Absence of second-hand smoke.** Exposure to smoke increases the risk of SIDS. Smoke does cling to hair and clothing. If you have smokers in your home or guest smokers, insist they smoke outside and request they change clothes or put a clean smock, jacket, or shirt over their clothes before holding an infant. Be assured, most child care providers do not allow infant caregivers who smoke and smoking is not allowed on the premises. This is one of the first questions you should ask if you are touring with your new grand infant.

- **Safe sleep place.** NO chairs, sofas, waterbeds, cushions, or adult beds. We all have allowed car seats, bouncy seats, and swings as a sleep place because the baby is *finally* asleep. Just know this is not best practice because baby heads tend to fall forward, and this reduces the intake of a full breath. Try it yourself and feel what happens. Make certain the appropriate crib, bassinet, or portable crib mattress is firm and tight-fitting to the crib. Make certain the sheet fits tightly over the mattress. Place the crib away from cords or ropes (such as blinds) as this is a strangulation hazard for standing babies.
- **Co-sleeping.** NOOOOOOO! Sleeping in the same bed or on the couch with your infant can increase the risk of SIDS and other dangers during sleep such as suffocation. The safest place for infants is in their own bassinet or crib placed close to you. There are products on the market like a side-car crib that can be attached to the side of your bed.
- **Baby monitors** have special sensors to track the babies' movement while they are sleeping and alert you to any stillness that may signal a problem. You can actually run and do the laundry or whatever you would do when not staring at the baby. Monitors also help reduce

stress and anxiety, so you might even get some sleep! Just make certain the electrical cords are three feet from the crib.

Cabinets

The most dangerous cabinet in the house is the medicine cabinet. Thank goodness someone invented the child-proof safety cap. Obviously, not a grandparent with a touch of arthritis in their hands. But this is a true safety necessity! In 1967, Dr. Henri J. Breault, a career pediatrician from Ontario, noticed ingestion of household medicines and other household products was causing the death or accidental injury in "global porportions." He decided he had to do something about it. He developed the "Palm N' Turn," and the incidence of child poisonings dropped by 91 percent.[2] The good news is my ten-year-old granddaughter can get these open for me. The bad news is my ten-year-old granddaughter can get these open. I also have to ask grands to read the teeny tiny print on the medicine directions. Not good when you have a screaming baby on your hip.

Prior to the invention of children's safety caps, I remember the day my daughter climbed up on the bathroom sink, opened the medicine cabinet, and saw the pretty pink baby aspirin bottle and

---

2   "Henri J. Breault, MD." Canadian Hall of Fame. Accessed March 20, 2019. http://www.cdnmedhall.org/inductees/henribreault.

ate nearly the whole thing. I noticed she was lying lethargically on the floor (this never happened), and I saw the bottle beside her. I called Poison Control and they told me to take her temperature. This was easier said than done. She then bit the thermometer in half and now had mercury in her mouth. So, I called Poison Control *again* and was told it was time to bring out the big guns: ipecac derived from the "road-side sick-making plant," ipecacuanha. Thank goodness I had it in the cabinet—the same cabinet where she'd found the baby aspirin. Maybe if she had grabbed the ipecac first it would have taught her a *real* lesson. Poison Control was my only "go-to" phone number as there was no 911 service available in our area at the time. It wasn't until 2001 that 97 percent of the US population had access to this life-saving service.

The most worrisome part of this problem is that many of today's medications simulate candy in color, size, shape, and desirability (gummy this, gummy that). If you have active toddlers or preschoolers, keep household medications in child-resistant containers, and in a high cabinet. Keep purses and briefcases with medications put away. Never refer to medications as "candy" or take your medications in front of them, and then leave it on the end table. Young children will imitate adults.

Sadly, it is not just the little children you have to worry about. That perfect teenager of yours may have pockets stuffed full with your blood pressure, anxiety, and pain medications to share with friends at the party that night. Or those friends might have asked to use your bathroom, and *their* pockets are stuffed full. The medicine cabinet is the primary source of drugs for twelve, thirteen, and fourteen-year-olds. Prescription medications and over-the-counter medication abuse is becoming the "thing." Some kids (and some adults) tend to think, "If a doctor says, 'it's okay,' it should be okay, right?" Wrong. "Pharm Parties" with bowls of "snack pills" are quite the rage. This is the prime opportunity to ask, "Would you jump off a bridge if _____ jumped?" Stress that these pills can cause death and pills don't pick and choose who they kill. *Please* have the "pills can kill you" talk."

Fire Safety

Would you know what to do in case of fire when you have grands in your home? Chances are good they have learned STOP, DROP, and ROLL in preschool or public schools. Chances are not so good families have discussed how to get out of the house in case of a fire. Have you? To be good at something, you have to practice. Take the time to discuss an escape plan and a meeting point.

You don't want to scare your grand, but make sure they know what dangers a fire can bring. Children aren't always aware of the consequences of their actions. There was a frightening day for us when our children were playing in a walk-in attic with a neighbor child. They were supposedly looking for a Sherriff's badge in a drawer. All fingers pointed to that neighbor when a fire started.

- Teach grands: DON'T PLAY with matches and lighters.
- Teach grands: STOP, DROP, and ROLL if the fire touches you.
- Teach grands to touch door knobs with a towel or clothing to see if hot.
- Teach grands: Get Down Low, and Go! Go! Go!
- Teach grands: DON'T HIDE! GO OUTSIDE!
- Teach grands to CALL 911 in case of fire once in a safe place.
- Teach your grand about fire safety and what they can do to prevent fires. The more they know, the less likely they are to cause an accident. Tour your local fire department with them and collect brochures. Our fire department lets children climb inside the fire truck and try on gear. An added plus is seeing a firefighter all suited up. Hopefully, a fire never happens, but knowing what a firefighter looks like could help take away the fear of a large, masked person coming into their bedroom.

This is not a one-time deal. You need to talk about and practice regularly. Despite all the "training," when asked, "What do you do in case of fire?" our five-year-old grand boy answered, "Grab some marshmallows."

**

Keeping your grandchildren safe is a full-time job. Your eyes cannot be everywhere at all times. Becoming a grandparent does not give you immediate super powers complete with great hearing skills, a wider peripheral vision, and the ability to be there with a safety net in the blink of an eye. We can only do what we can do. We just do it to the best of our ability—and more slowly than we used to.

"TRUST YOURSELF. YOU KNOW MORE
THAN YOU THINK YOU DO."
—DR. BENJAMIN SPOCK

CHAPTER 6

Technology Takeover

There is a new foreign language my grandchildren speak that I just don't get. Social media and texting ... whatever. I am coming around. On the other hand, I am a charter member of the original chat room: the telephone party line. Try explaining to your grands how you shared your telephone line with four, six, or eight other families. Their first question was, "You mean other people could hear you talking to your *boy*friend?" I couldn't resist saying, "Well, yes. Just like that teenager in line at Taco Bell, talking to *her* boyfriend all kissy kissy on the cellphone!"

The Dark Ages could well describe where I live in this new world. I do have a "little phone," as my husband calls it, but he will be the last man on earth to own one. He does ask for me to look up directions sometimes, but gets mad when I can't figure it out. At least I am trying! When attending a women in business conference recently, we were asked to stand to designate when we had purchased various technology. I was the last woman to stand as I had just gotten my first cellphone when I sold my centers (no need for one when you are at work ten-hours-a-day with a land line!). When asked what kind I had, my response was "pink." Even though I have had it for a while now, I still can't figure the thing out. Once I had to run out of a funeral service because I didn't know how to turn the ringer off. Do you feel my pain?

Can't get the TV remote to work? Do you ever click your computer keys until you lose your letter to the editor into Neverland—never to be seen again? Or where did that video go on your cellphone that you just took of your grand's first step? Good news! This is what you have grandchildren for! *My* personal techno geek (oldest grandson) lives within ten minutes and can drive now, so talk about quick service calls. Feed him some nachos and cheese, and he is good to go. Big problem—he leaves for college soon. We have encouraged him to go with the understanding that he will still be accessible for technology fallouts. My husband said he hopes it doesn't cost $$$ to call our grand at college. I reminded my husband that if he had his own cellphone, it wouldn't.

I am not too worried, because I have some up and comers. There is the two-year-old who got onto my son's phone, kept on clicking, and (accidentally) hired an Uber. After seeing a black car parked out in front of the house for fifteen minutes, son No. 2 considered calling the police, but went to double check first. The mystery was solved when he remembered his daughter had been playing with the cellphone. Bad news—he still had to pay the Uber driver (he said fortunately it was the cheaper one. Ha!) Then there are the five-to eight-year-olds who can find any American Girl Doll or Barbie YouTube video ever made. I'm going to need their help soon so I try to stay on their good side.

So, here is the downside of today's technology takeover: isolation. If you can't remember what color your grand's eyes are because they are always staring at some sort of screen, it's time to set some guidelines.

I have real concerns about how technology is changing social and communication skills, as well as creating an actual addiction. Did you know that according to Vision Critical, Generation Z uses their smartphones 15.4 hours per week—more than any other type of device? That Gen Z consumes 13.2 hours of TV content per week? That they "prefer cool products over cool experiences"? Generation Z is the first to be born after 1995, into a time when technology is rampant. They are entrepreneurial and tech savvy.[3] Do you spend your time saying, "Turn off that computer?" "Turn off that TV?" Can you see how social media is making children *less* social? Tablets, ear buds, and smartphones are definitely affecting hearing and replacing conversation. TV shows and advertisements feature families around the dinner table, on the couch, or room to room, communicating by text.

Have you witnessed families at a restaurant where everyone is eyes-down with a device on their lap? I was in a buffet-style restaurant recently where a father-daughter dinner was taking place. I guessed it was a dad who maybe had his seven- or eight-year-old daughter for the weekend. Doesn't matter. The entire time he was on his cellphone. She got up several times to hit the buffet line and he never ate, he never looked up. What a lost opportunity for the dad. I thought about getting up to sit and talk with her myself, but didn't. Another lost opportunity. These behaviors negatively impact social interaction *in real life*. This is reflected in group interactions (or lack thereof) in school and work. Many children and young adults don't know how to navigate conversations, problem solve, or even work together for a common mission. Plus, the internet

---

3   Kleinschmit, Matt. "Generation Z Characteristics: 5 Infographics on the Gen Z Lifestyle." Vision Critical. Vision Critical Communications, Inc., October 7, 2019. https://www.visioncritical.com/blog/generation-z-infographics.

and social media are not always wholesome. Consider purchasing approved parental control software that blocks unsuitable websites while keeping you in the know about which sites they are visiting, and which words and phrases your kids are searching.

Technology is not only creating social problems, it is causing physical problems as well. Teens should do sixty minutes or more of moderate-to-vigorous activity every single day. The minimum is thirty minutes, three times a week. If kids are on a device ten hours-per-day, guess what? That isn't happening. You have a slouch potato. Exactly. Fitness levels continue to drop as children choose sedentary lifestyles, playing interactive games on the computer or watching videos over going outside to ride a bike, kick a ball, or engage with friends.

As an early childhood educator, I have witnessed how obesity has increased in children at younger ages. The World Health Organization reported this number has increased tenfold in ages five through nineteen in the last forty years. I assure you that it starts earlier than five. I suspect some parents try to keep their children in after-school activities, specifically for this needed exercise and away from technology. Latch-key kids are a different story. Snacks and technology galore. I understand this may be the best solution for the family, but expect consequences.

Online references and smart speakers are replacing dictionaries and encyclopedias. When I was in eighth grade, all I wanted for Christmas was a World Book Encyclopedia set. This was a big ask. I don't know how my divorced, no-alimony, no-child-support mom did it, but I got that encyclopedia set. I spent hours flipping pages to see all the places I wanted to go, people I wished I could meet. Now you can just go to Wikipedia or ask Siri. But how do you even know what to ask without flipping pages? When telling this story (usually at Christmas), I have had a few grands ask me, "what is an encyclopedia?" I was even more astonished on a homework helping day when my grand didn't know how to use a dictionary. I felt like I should be bringing out my oil lamp and quill pen.

On the other hand, I have actually learned to enjoy texting because I can send my thoughts, prayers, and questions out at 2 a.m. when I can't sleep, *and* I usually get a response ... someday. But texting has also become a too-easy way to communicate negative thoughts and feelings twenty-four hours a day without eye-to-eye, face-to-face contact. Texting creates an opportunity for open-season for bullying. In addition, with no tone, often even positive words may be misconstrued.

R Rated: For Mature Audiences Only. Sexting is so far out of my time zone, I just don't get it. Sexting is sending explicit images through smartphones, the internet, and other devices. According to *JAMA Pediatrics*, February 2018, one in seven teens reports sending sexts, and one in four reports receiving them.[4] With access to personal smartphones and Snapchat, this is on the increase. Normal curiosity and flirtation are natural behaviors. Sexting, however, may make girls feel pressured to participate and worry about being a prude if they don't. Boys tend to look at it as social status. Then, when there is the big breakup, there is the danger of the photos going viral. Classmates can be cruel. Everyone should post only what they are comfortable with the whole world seeing. Once it is out there—and it is out there, you can't take it back. These images are impossible to delete. As embarrassing as it was in our day, this is so many levels beyond boys boasting in the locker room.

CAUTION: Predators are lurking out there everywhere, easily cropping and moving innocent photos posted on social media to adult sites, and worse, the Dark Net. I was constantly approached by parents to put cameras in my centers so they could watch their child's daily activities on the

4   Madigan, Sheri, Anh L. Ly, and Christina L. Rash. "Prevalence of Multiple Forms of Sexting Behavior Among Youth: A Systematic Review and Meta-Analysis." JAMA Network, April 2018. https://jamanetwork.com/journals/jamapediatrics/fullarticle/2673719.

internet. Never! I learned early on how easily a predator could hack into these videos. I had too many two-year-old potty training kiddos running around with bare bums to risk their privacy.

Grandparents: Think twice before you post those adorable bubble bath photos online. Think twice before you post something that shares personal or identifying information that shows intimate knowledge of the child or teen (bedroom photo, vanity license tag, etc.). Online luring is real. It happened to one of my teachers' thirteen-year-old daughters right here in Smalltown, USA. Discuss with teens appropriate and inappropriate postings and get teens' permission before you post. Once it is out there, it is out there and you can't take it back.

Don't get me wrong. There is definitely a place in today's fast-paced society for these devices. This is after your grand has learned the art of small talk beyond, "How was your day at school?" After your grand has gone on a nature walk with you and possibly made a collage of treasures found. After mealtime.

I know the drill. Kids can whine you into submission. Some days, *you* need the break, and it is just easier to give in for fifteen minutes (or an hour) of peace and quiet. But do you feel like technology is taking over your life? Robbing you of time with your grandchildren? Interfering with the imagination of childhood?

- **There is a time and place for using a device for learning—but only fifteen-to-thirty minutes a day.** There are some great programs for math and reading skills. Moderation is the key. This is not to be a replacement for how children really learn through the experience of play and interaction with other children and adults. Many school systems have taken books out of their hands and replaced with books on computers. Time to step up and Nana! Read real books with your grands! I know firsthand how the new math is beyond confusing. Get out your pennies and show your grands how it works. You might as well go ahead and teach them how to tell time on an analog clock or write their signature in cursive, because those things are no longer in some school curriculums either.

- **Devices can be over stimulating.** Long before addiction occurs, our little one's brain can short-circuit, allowing stress to set in. Red flags can be meltdowns over nothing, rage, defiance when told to shut down the device, "wired and tired." Children are constantly being entertained, so they *need* to be entertained. Reset by taking away technology—completely. Not just a cutback. This is not a punishment.

This is giving the brain a rest from sensory overload. This is giving them a chance to learn how to entertain themselves.

- **Restaurants are not the place for devices.** Your grand will learn to associate meal time with technology and never experience the enjoyment of socializing over a meal. "Let's do lunch" may become a thing of the past. Tic-tac-toe and Hangman on a paper napkin have helped us through many of those long waits for their chicken nuggets. (Yes, no matter how fancy the restaurant they will still order chicken nuggets. That's okay!) Children need the experience of eating properly in public and on a white tablecloth with a real napkin. Too bad we don't have Manners the Butler from the 1958 television ad to pick up those slippery napkins as they are bound to land on the floor.

- **Children will mimic adult behavior.** I had two little grands walking out the door to the mailbox with play phones in their hands. I asked, "What's with the phones?" and their simultaneous response was "Mommy does this." Hmmm.

- **If you notice your grands are constantly waiting for data to come in—scrolling, listening for the next ding—chances are good they are not learning to notice social cues around them.** Have you ever picked up your pocketbook and no one looks up to notice you are ready to go? You say, "Nana is leaving" and no one looks up? Time for an intervention!

- **It is your job to help your grands make wise choices, to set family rules, and what the consequences will be if the rules are not followed.** You need to teach your grands the value of relationships and respect for your expectations in your home. Technology at my house is always pre-approved. And there is no technology behind closed doors. And "turn it off!" is not a negotiation. Children may be good kids, but they don't always make good choices.

- **It is your job to help Generation Z incorporate their social media obsession into a balanced, healthy, whole life.** Cellphones have already replaced watches, cameras, calendars, calculators, and alarm clocks. Please don't let them replace your family.

"IF WE DO NOT TEACH OUR CHILDREN SOCIETY WILL. AND THEY—AND WE—WILL HAVE TO LIVE WITH THE RESULTS."

—STEPHEN COVEY

CHAPTER 7

Terrible Twos ... Oops, Teens

Teens and terrible twos both push boundaries and throw tantrums. Both are in the process of pulling away from adults and asserting their own independence. They both think they are the center of the universe. Grandparenting a teen can be stressful, frustrating, and heartbreaking. I feel like saying, "I changed your diaper! Get over yourself!"

Teenagers are baffling. In one minute (day, week, month) they are simultaneously moody, defiant, reckless, impulsive, and argumentative. The rolling of eyes and slamming of doors is jarring. Just when you get used to this, they show up at your door with a bouquet of flowers—just because. Be assured, this is normal teen behavior.

Brain Development. The part of the brain to manage emotions, make decisions, and control inhibitions is simply not developed yet. To paraphrase Molly Edmonds, in her article, "Are teenage brains really different from adult brains?" at this stage, there are loose wires everywhere. It is like the entertainment center speakers are not connected to the DVD player and the DVD player is not connected to the TV and they can't find the remote control at all.[5]

Synapses are forming at the speed of lightning, but the whole brain will not reach full maturity until the mid-twenties. There is only *their* world and you may not be in it that day. Even though your teen grands may be taller than you and appear mature, they are not thinking as adults. I have seen the "glazed-eyed look" plenty of times, and can almost hear the wheels turning, but I can't count on the result I want.

Disconnect From Reality

Social media may cause the apocalypse, the end of the world as we know it. Just kidding! But to teens, that smartphone is an appendage. It is a great way to connect, but teens are forgetting how to disconnect instead. Research shows that being addicted to social media is having negative

---

[5]   Edmonds, Molly. "Are Teenage Brains Really Different from Adult Brains?" How Stuff Works. InfoSpace Holdings, LLC, August 26, 2008. https://science. howstuffworks.com/life/inside-the-mind/human-brain/teenage-brain1.htm.

effects on teens as is seen in low self-esteem, sleep deprivation, anxiety, and depression. Social media sites can create a false sense of reality as teens watch exciting things other friends have done (so they say). You may notice selfies are always taken when they are on their coolest road trip, with their whitest teeth, and no blemishes. Photo editing apps to the rescue! But what does this say about who they really are? Who they *think* they really are? Each and every day, the line is blurring between internet reality and real-life reality. Back in the day, popularity was determined by how many votes you got for Prom King or Queen. Today it is how many followers you have. And these teens keep count.

Social Skills

Do teens even have social skills anymore? One thing for sure, they must be taught. It is not an inherited trait. This is on us.

- **Etiquette: (structure within which manners operate)** My grandmother would put on her pearls, ask my brothers and me to get on our Sunday church clothes, and head to the dining room—the *real* dining room—whenever she came to visit. There was a white tablecloth, and the silverware and glasses were laid out like a state dinner at the White House. The boys pulled out my chair and then with napkins on lap, we began the meal after our hostess had picked up her fork. Conversation was an important and energetic part of this meal. "May I be excused?" was expected when adult time began. I have yet to be invited to the White House for dinner, but I will be ready when it happens. "May I, please?" and "Thank you" need to be modeled. At age four, our grands are expected to start ordering their own meal at a restaurant or fast food place. "May I please" better be the first thing out of their mouths. Boys walking on the street side of the sidewalk and opening the door for ladies is a *must* for our generation, but this has gotten lost along the way as many young women don't want or expect it. Darn that women's lib thing we fought so hard for. It is still worth a try with your teens!

- **Manners: (how you behave toward other people, consideration, kindness)** Don't even get me started on manners. Where have they gone? Didn't you just want to live in Mr. Rogers' Neighborhood where everyone was kind, polite, respectful, and had manners? Check out www.neighborhoodarchive.com for a reminder of manners your grands need to be taught or reminded about. And Emily Post sure would be disappointed not to receive a thank you note for the birthday present, Christmas gift, or graduation money she sent. Even invitations these days are sent through the internet and responds are requested on a website. I think I have read more "Dear Abby" letters from grandparents about this topic than anything else. I send thank-you notes for *everything* in hopes the point will be taken. Wanting to look cool doesn't mean you can forget your manners. Asking permission, saying, "excuse me," apologizing, and not interrupting are definitely still "cool" to me. Not shoveling food into their mouths is a bonus. Cellphone manners are a whole new ballgame. I say leave them in the glove compartment when you come to my house. Of course your teen will ask, "What is a glove compartment?"

- **Communication Skills:** PUT DOWN THE PHONE! Make eye contact! Teens need to learn how to engage in meaningful conversation. In my experience, most teens are not forthcoming or conversation starters outside of their friend circle. Take your teen out to lunch or dinner for quality one-on-one time with no other siblings. While you have their attention, ask open-ended questions. You will be amazed what an interesting young adult is sitting there with you eating breadsticks at Olive Garden. On one of my grandson's college tours, the university proudly announced there was a life skills course that included how to talk to someone in an elevator. Really?

Entitled Age

No matter what they get, they want more and need it now. Everything is happening at warp speed, a tap of a finger. Television and the internet bombard teens with gadgets they must have now! We see our own children working hard and stressed out, trying to keep up with the Joneses. They are too exhausted and overwhelmed, and it is just easier to give in to kids' demands. This is nothing new. It is just on a much, much bigger scale. Parents living vicariously through your grands is exhausting—violin, gymnastics, soccer, ice skating, golf, whatever. There are not enough hours in the day. The Nana van is rolling and can't make one more stop!

Back to being entitled, what's with participation trophies for all these activities? Everyone is a winner? For just showing up? Where is *my* trophy? I show up. Overcoming failure and mistakes would make kids and teens stronger and help them learn it takes time to get good at something. They can't win every time. They can't get a trophy every time. Well, apparently some parents think they can. It was a sad day when my fourteen-year-old grand boy practiced almost daily for a year, traveled over 700 miles to a national sport shooting competition; he won the silver individually and the team won fourth overall. Picture time came around and a team member's mom came over and took that well-deserved silver trophy right out of his hands and handed it to a teammate to hold for the team photo. He was so stunned, he couldn't react in time to right the wrong and the photo was snapped. In his mind he had worked a long time to have someone else acknowledged for his dedication. He is respectful of adults but assures me next time, he will not let go of that trophy.

It is natural for parents and grandparents to want our children to have what we didn't have. To do what we didn't do. Grandparents feel good that we can give our time and money now. But real life is not easy. Be cautious you aren't contributing to creating a spoiled, ungrateful, entitled brat.

Disrespectful Behavior:
Unfortunately, this comes with the territory. Moving between childhood and adulthood and seeking healthy independence can lead to mild (or not so mild) disrespect. Teens lack the emotional maturity they need to make informed decisions. I have been fortunate not to experience this personally with my own grands, but have witnessed it big-time out in public. The Japanese have this down pat. They even have a "Respect for the Aged Day" to celebrate their elders and have a "no elderly-left-behind" attitude. I need to write a letter to someone about that!

So, how do we deal with this disrespectful behavior? I guarantee, if asked, the teens would say *we* are not respecting *them*—their privacy for sure. They don't always understand that simply because we don't agree with them does not mean we do not respect them. Respect has to be earned on both sides. It is how you treat your grand while making decisions and enforcing rules that makes a difference. Random House Webster's College Dictionary defines respect as "a proper acceptance or courtesy; respect for the elderly."[6] Two-way street.

- **Don't take it personally.** Eye rolling, ignored requests, stomping feet. Sound like that Terrible Twos stage? Yep, here we go again.
- **Establish ground rules and boundaries. Be consistent.** Nana and PopPop, you must set your house rules together—and stick to your guns. From the beginning of time, children have played adults one against the other. How many times did *you* say, "What did your father/ mother say?"
- **Enforce consequences.** Does it seem like nothing is working? As James Lehman says, "You can't punish your child into better behavior."[7]

6   "Respect." In Random House Webster's College Dictionary, 1147. New York, NY: Random House, 1991.
7   Lehman, James. "How to Give Kids Consequences That Work." Empowering Parents. Accessed March 20, 2019. https://www.empoweringparents.com/article/how-to-give-kids-consequences-that-work/.

Grounding, taking away video games, or taking away car keys doesn't always work. Identify and discuss the behavior you want to change. Come up with a list of privileges and consequences together. Encourage your grand to exhibit self-control and practice better behavior for a period of time with the ability to earn the privileges back. Acknowledge good behavior, but make certain they know there will be consequences for bad behavior.

Consequences should be related to behavior that needs to be changed. Be task specific. Show physical examples. If the problem is a messy room with mile-high laundry, don't just point out the hamper. Have your teen pick up strewn items and determine if they are clean or dirty. If they are dirty, tell your teen to take them to the laundry. Put them in charge of not only taking theirs to the laundry room, but also taking the entire family's laundry.

Consequences should not be too harsh, but something they will really miss. Young teens are still attached to baby dolls and blankies. For others, it will be their cellphone, video game, or computer. Too harsh? Maybe. You know your grand.

Consequences should be short-term, but long enough to see improvement. Try to avoid saying, "You're grounded for life!"

- **Don't threaten and fail to act.** Worst mistake ever. Why should they bother? Why will they listen in the future?
- **Don't say, "I told you this was going to happen."** This will only make your teen angry.
- **Communicate.** I say Step No. 1 is to feed your teen. They are always hungry and working up to hangry. Then, maybe talk while you walk, shoot baskets, or kick a soccer ball. Interrogation under the bright light does not work with teens. Emphatic finger pointing over the dinner table eye-to-eye does not work with teens. They will shut down and shut you out in a heartbeat. Plan a specific time to sit together and talk. Be willing to listen, remain calm, and acknowledge their feelings. Follow up—later. Hours, days, weeks may be needed to process.
- **Focus on the positive.** Stay calm, compliment good decisions. Rewarding works better than punishing. In one word: incentives! FYI, incentives do not always equate to things or money. Time and activities can outweigh a gift card. According to Joseph Allen, University of Virginia, "Rewards give them something they want to think about. Punishment is something they don't want to think about." Hard work is rewarded. This is not a bribe.
- **Let them take healthy risks.** This leads to higher self-esteem, confidence, and they are even more

likely to attend college and become law-abiding adults. Aren't there some things you will never share from your high school days? And you are alive to tell about it? Not all risk-taking is bad. Statistics show 40 percent of teens will try drugs once. But 60 percent will not. Half of teens will experiment with alcohol, but half will not. Mine better be in the *not*. This is certainly one area where very specific consequences need to be determined ASAP.

- **Don't sweat the small stuff.** Pick your battles. Some things aren't worth the argument—unless bleeding is involved.
- **Do things together.**
  - *Jurassic Park* movie night and I am there!
  - Amusement Park. I will have to watch this one from afar, but will have my camera ready.
  - White water rafting, hiking—but no camping—Hampton Inn, please. I have points for that.
  - Participate in a walk-a-thon, visit a nursing home, make cotton candy at a festival to save the whales. What better way to teach about giving back to the community?
  - Board games. Chess takes hours, but it's quality conversation time.
  - ROAD TRIP! Try new foods, meet new people, get lost.

- Let them decide what to do. Learn something new about them and go forward with a smile on your face—even if there is fear in your heart.

Why do I love my teenagers? The babies are getting all the ooohs and aaahs, and I certainly need my baby fix. The tweens still love to play Simon Says and I Spy with My Little Eye" with the preschoolers.

But these teens!

They are so funny! Jokes, tricks, and sarcasm. They get it.

- They don't watch Nickelodeon 24/7 (I am beginning to think of the *iCarly* cast as my extended family).
- They sleeeep. Peace. And. Quiet.
- They feed, shower, and dress themselves. And their clothes match.
- They do chores. Real chores that my body can't reach, lift, or bend to do.
- They travel lightly. Just a change of undies, and we are good to go.
- They drive me to the store, and don't beg for candy at check out.
- And their *hugs*. In their busy, busy lives they still make me feel like the most special Nana in the world. Even if it isn't cool.

"TEENAGERS ARE THE MOST
MISUNDERSTOOD PEOPLE ON THE PLANET.
THEY ARE TREATED LIKE CHILDREN AND
EXPECTED TO ACT LIKE ADULTS."

–ANONYMOUS

CHAPTER 8

The Little Engine That Could

THE MAGIC OF READING ... OR NOT!

My favorite "heart-warming" moments with my grands are snuggling up in a cozy place and reading (for the thousandth time) some of their "forever favorite" books. Going to the library opens up a whole new world. You can snuggle there, also! Reading is our time tunnel to another world. Reading is an escape for so many of our little ones into imaginary places where life does not hurt quite so badly. Reading is my personal "Calgon, take me away" moment!

Our house is full of books. Fiction and non-fiction. Classics from when I was teaching a hundred years ago (*Stone Soup*, *Millions of Cats*, *Mike Mulligan's Steam Shovel*) newer books from my child development days (*Goodnight Moon*,

Stellaluna) and even the free ones we get in kids' meals from Chick-fil-A. Caldecott Award winners (*Where the Wild Things Are, Make Way for Ducklings*) are front and center. I love, love going back in time to books with thought-provoking question opportunities like, *The Little Rabbit Who Wanted Red Wings.* But my all-time favorite might just be *The Little Engine That Could,* published in 1930 and written by Watty Piper. This story teaches the value of optimism and hard work. I often use this book, as well as *Oh, The Places You'll Go* by Dr. Seuss as gifts for graduates or for people of all ages who are starting a new phase in their lives.

When you read with your grand, something magical happens. Imaginations soar, vocabulary increases, and comprehension grows. And, hopefully, a lifelong love of reading begins. We often stop and discuss concepts, new words and ask questions. Not just yes and no questions. Open-ended questions. What do you think is going to happen next? Why? When? How? Questions instill curiosity and allow your grand to be a part of the story. Ask about the illustrations and how they relate to the story. Talk about the front cover, back cover, spine, and title page. Talk about the author and illustrator. For beginning readers, point to each word as you go. Bring out your inner child and read with goofy voices, inflection, and emphasis on exclamation points and question marks. Children will mimic your style in their own storytelling and reading. And I guarantee your grand has that "forever favorite" book memorized, so you best read EVERY ... SINGLE ... WORD ... or they will call you on it!

A child's brain develops faster from birth to age three than at any other point of their lives, forming more than one million new neural connections every second. Reading to your grands nurtures their brains and lays a foundation for healthy learning development. Reading together provides not only academic but emotional benefits, and children will be less likely to be hyperactive or disruptive. Everything you say and do affects their growth. It is easier to shape a three-year-old than fix a middle-aged man. No pressure. Just be aware.

Here comes the hard part. Some children are born readers and some are *not*. They haven't discovered the magic. What do you do when it is homework time and all you hear is "I HATE reading!"? And then you get the face, the aaaggghh, the rolling on the floor in agony. Counting how many pages are left in the chapter ten times. They loved those snuggle up times with you but for *them* to read by themselves is not happening. Reading is a proactive activity. Children today are so used to being reactive to the world around them that reading may be a challenge, frustrating, and just not fun. Several reasons a child might not enjoy reading independently:

- **Every child develops at his or her own pace.** Some children might not yet be confident in their speech, language, and sounds. The phonetic reading we grew up with in the past has been replaced with "sight words." This requires out-of-context memorization. Tall order for a short kid! Write the sight words on note cards, rocks, blocks, etc., and help your grand build sentences. Make those words meaningful.

- **They just haven't found an interesting topic.** Allow your grand to select the book. Reread many times the books you discover they do like to read. I have one grandson who read the entire *Harry Potter* series in the second grade. It caught his imagination. But the others, not so much. Have them write their own books/journals with photos of family and favorite places, trips, and events they have enjoyed. They will be proud to read these books to everyone and anyone. Now *you* might not be able to read them. Younger children tend to use "Driting" (drawing + writing), which is a combination of drawing, squiggles, some letters, some numbers, and some real words. This is an important developmental step, so go with the flow. Have you seen the T-shirts that say, *"ef yoo kan rid* *ths yoo prbli ar a teecha"?* (Some grandparents can read these magical words. Can you?)

- **Books are not on their minds.** Books stored in a closet are not going to get read. Create a special place for books or even a reading nook, so if the mood swings, they know where to go. I am not ashamed to admit we have a basket of books next to every toilet in the house. When you have a captive audience, take advantage!

- **Sitting still**. The wiggles are going to come out one way or another. Be creative in where and how your grand reads. Go to the library when the *Star Wars* characters are there and have photos taken. Or go when it is Therapy Dog Day—petting calms and brings smiles. Then find a cozy corner and snuggle down at the library to read! Just know, it is okay to stand up. It is okay to go outside and sit on the porch swing and kick legs. It is okay to go to the park and stick feet in the sandbox (very calming for children with sensory issues). It is okay to read through a magnifying glass to help with focus. Supporting story props like stuffed animals, puppets, trucks, and dolls can reinforce the story line and help your grand gain confidence. Even older children will enjoy being in charge of the bell while reading *The Polar Express*.

- **Timing.** There are times when a child *will* be receptive to reading. But I have learned this is *not* as soon as they get off the school bus and have not had a snack. That just leads to the "hangrys" (hungry/angry). It is not when everyone else in the neighborhood is jumping on the trampoline in the backyard. Our favorite time is bedtime. Baths are done, teeth are brushed, and lights are low. Best time of the day!

- **Adults around them are not reading.** It is important for you to read for pleasure yourself. This could be reading the morning newspaper over breakfast. This could be sitting on the beach while they play in the tidal pool. This does *not* mean always reading an e-book. Working or checking your email does not count either. Your grand needs to see you with a real book in your hand, respecting that book. No bending of corners!

- **Testing.** The US public school system has managed to take away the pure joy of leisure reading. Plus, there is no time for it. Parent and teacher concerns about teaching to the test run rampant. There are computer tests at the end of every weekly reading book. There are tests at the end of each daily passage that are in such a teeny tiny type size, my grand girl had to get reading glasses. There are EOGs (those dreaded End of Grade Tests) that cause nausea and panic attacks.

One grand girl was excited to read one of my *Nancy Drew* books, *The Clue of the Leaning Chimney*, over spring break because it is inscribed from *my* grandmother in 1959 for my eleventh birthday—and she was turning eleven. The teacher said the reading level was not high enough so "it wouldn't count" and she would have to read a second book. So, only certain books qualify.

When I taught elementary in the '70s, we had individualized reading, which was tough to manage, but the children *loved* to read! They brought in motorcycle magazines, *Field and Stream, Highlights*, "forever favorites"— whatever. I didn't care if they brought in the Sears Christmas Wish Book. Once non-readers learn to read and love to read, they can then move on to those books that "count."

Don't give up! Don't let them give up! No matter the age, read *The Little Engine That Could*. "I think I can, I think I can, I think I can," could become, "I thought I could, I thought I could, I thought I could."

***

Inspiring children to love to read has become a mission of Dolly Parton's.

She believes "Every book is a treasure and every time you open one up, you will meet new friends and take wonderful journeys to magical places. There is no limit to what you can do or how far you go. Just remember the lessons my family taught me—dream big dreams; learn everything you can learn; and care for all those who care for you. You do all of these things and you can be anyone you want to be."

Dolly Parton created Dolly Parton's Imagination Library as a tribute to her "Daddy." "He was the smartest man I have ever known," she says, "but I know in my heart his inability to read probably kept him from fulfilling all of his dreams." Her dream is that all children will grow up in a home full of books.

The Imagination Library is a book-gifting program launched in 1995 that mails high-quality, age-appropriate books to children from birth until Kindergarten no matter the family's income. One of my grands recently received Dolly Parton's, *Coat of Many Colors*, and it has quickly become a family favorite and passed from cousin to cousin. Check out *www.imaginationlibrary.com* to see if your community participates in this program.[8]

---

8   All Dolly Parton quotes are from www.ImaginationLibrary.com and used with permission from The Dollywood Foundation.

"YOU CAN NEVER GET ENOUGH BOOKS INTO
THE HANDS OF ENOUGH CHILDREN."

"THE FIRST STEP IS ALWAYS THE HARDEST,
BUT YOU'LL NEVER KNOW UNLESS YOU TRY."
–DOLLY PARTON

CHAPTER 9

Frequent Flyer Miles

GRANDPARENTING FROM A DISTANCE

So, you can't be there in person. It will be okay. Love between grandparents and grandchildren knows no distance, but it *is* sometimes sad. Two of our grands were born California girls and California is a *long* way from North Carolina. Missing their births was probably hardest for us as there was no quick way to travel 3,000 miles and get to that birthing room on time. PopPop and I grabbed the red-eye ASAP, eager to meet our first precious California prize! As important as that trip was, it was tough on our "not young anymore" bodies. Because of the distance, visits weren't simply a jump in the car, so there was serious planning involved for all future trips coast to coast. By the time our second California girl was born, we knew what we were doing. And, fortunately, No. 1 son and his wife traveled frequently for work, and their trips east made our visits more frequent. This was a perfect plan until one grand turned two years old, and an airline ticket had to be purchased! I gotta admit, the best news ever was when they were transferred back to the Tar Heel State after five years! The MacPac was out in full force with "Welcome Home" signs and lots of tears when our surfer dude and his family came down the airport escalator.

We are the fortunate grandparents, having the entire MacPac clan within thirty minutes, but our grands' *other* grandparents live in states many, many miles away. I admit to feeling guilty sometimes because I get to experience so much of our grands' daily lives, so when the long-distance grandparents visit, PopPop and I step back and let them have their special time. We have learned how to share and play well with others, and it is worth it to see the smiles on their faces.

I admire our grands' other grandparents who burn up the highway to travel through four states, 500-plus miles, and more than seven hours to watch our grand girls in a dance recital that lasts three minutes. I admire our grands' other grandparents who fly in from 1,200 miles away to surprise our grandson with a visit from his cousin he sees only a few times a year. I admire our grands' other grandparents who instill the importance of their family history by coordinating events on the generational family farm. This is what long-distance grandparents do.

Thanks to new technology and express mail, long-distance grandparents can find ways to stay connected to grands on another coastline, in another state, or even in another country. Word of advice, if your grand does live in another country: *please* make an effort to learn the language, customs, traditions, and culture. This is their life. When your five-year-old grand visits from Japan and asks for sushi for lunch, you will be prepared! Visit local cultural events that will give you a better understanding of food, activities, and celebrations your grand is experiencing. Visiting Japan will be a lot easier if you know when to bow and when *not* to shake hands.

The snail mail we used with our own grandparents took forever. Plus we had to pay extra for Airmail envelopes! But today, sending cards, hand-written letters, or a small gift in the mail is quicker and gives grands something to hold onto and keep forever—maybe in a special box—and everyone enjoys receiving "love stuff!"

The best Grandparents' Day gift we ever made at my child development centers was an outline of the child's hands cut out of construction paper and attached to another long strip of construction paper on each end. These hands were to wrap a *big* hug around the grandparent. How about if you reverse that gift, cut out shapes of your own handprints, and mail *your* hug to them? They can also place your handprint over their heart and feel you are there. When they are older and open that special box with all these treasures, they will realize you were thinking about them across the miles, even though they couldn't see you.

Speaking of seeing, using video chats can easily bridge the distance between you and your grands. I know. I know. This is not the same as snuggling, hugging, and kissing—the real deals. But if you have a computer, a tablet, or a smartphone, this technology is fast, real time, and free. For those of us still technologically challenged, there are even new tablets designed specifically for seniors. They don't have the clutter and distractions of other stuff we don't need or want just to video chat with our grands.

- Schedule a designated weekly time to chat and put it on your calendar! Eight out of our ten grands are proficient enough to call on their own at other times when they need that special connection! Believe me, they all know how to find their parents' cellphones.
- While video chatting, play games (Peek-a-Boo, Old Maid, Simon Says); sing songs ("Head and Shoulders, Knees, and Toes"); read books and tell stories. Select books and stories about things they are currently doing like gymnastics,

soccer, or going to kindergarten or even to the dentist. This lets them know you are thinking about them and keeps you a part of their day. Buy two copies of the books and send one to your grands so you are reading together.

- Dress for the occasion! If it is a birthday Skype/Facetime call, wear a birthday hat and have a cupcake in your hand with a candle for your grand to "blow" out. Super Bowl Sunday, wear your favorite team jersey. If your grand is at the beach, don your sun hat and sunglasses, and call with a lemonade in your hand and your best "Wish I was there" smile. For prom night, well, just do the best you can. I know I can't fit in *my* prom dress!

- Set up your iPad or computer on the kitchen table and eat dinner together. Make clear this is the exception to the rule. A special meal with Nana and PopPop is different than playing Minecraft at the table. Attend a ball game together and high-five when the team scores. Take a nature walk together, and collect treasures. Call out their spelling words for their big test on Friday. The sky is the limit! Maybe that is why it is called Skype!

**Time for a *real* visit? Face to Face? *Real*
snuggles, hugs, and kisses? Woo-hoo!**

- **So, they are coming to *you* for two weeks this
  summer?** If your grands haven't visited you in
  a while, try to make your home as familiar and
  child-friendly as possible. Make certain that
  photos of them, their parents, siblings, and pets
  are on your refrigerator and around the house
  to help make some connections. Have those
  chocolate chip cookies you ship to them ready
  to eat (no matter what time they arrive). Pull
  out toys Mom or Dad played with—anything
  Fisher-Price will do—and share stories about
  their parents and their childhood.

I have a dedicated toy closet filled with photo-
labeled plastic tubs (for faster clean-up). The labels
include dress up; puzzles; play dishes; pots, pans,
and food; art supplies (pipe cleaners are the BEST);
blocks; plastic animals; stuffed animals; trucks
and cars; bean bags (make a cornhole game with
just a circle on a piece of cardboard); plus games,
footballs, soccer balls, basketballs, and croquet.

Forewarned is forearmed ... tiny toys and
barefeet don't mix. I must admit, sometimes I get
just plain tired and have to say, "Go to the closet."
Works for them. Works for me. A couple of my
grands worked hard straightening up the closet
after one rowdy session. They made a sign for the

door: "PUT TOYS BACK WHERE YOU GOT IT. THANK YOU!" Grammatically, this was not correct, but I guess I have trained them well.

After a busy day at the park; the nature museum or planetarium (thank goodness for annual memberships); the Friday night concert and dance; or a bike ride to watch the sunset, it is definitely TV time. I am okay with that. But one of our biggest challenges is Nana and PopPop don't have all those fancy TV channels and options they have at home. "Just pause it, Nana" doesn't work here. We go to the DVD store and rent some movies for fifty cents together as I haven't figured out Redbox either. Thank goodness we do get the channel "The Golden Girls" is on as that is a real favorite. My grand girls think it is hysterical, but they worry about the one GG who goes on too many dates.

My biggest piece of advice for when grands visit you? Don't think you are going to make a schedule and it is going to happen. Go with the flow, and allow your grands to be part of your planning. All will be well. At the end of the day, you will put your feet up and wonder, just as I do, "When do their parents eat or take a bath?"

- So, you are going to *their house*? Well, this is a whole different story. The No. 1 rule is discuss the length of your visit in advance to not overstay your welcome. For some families, a long weekend may be plenty of together time. For others, a week or two weeks might be great! Especially if you have traveled a long distance. No. 2 rule is to remember to bite your tongue, zip your lip. Their house, their rules. You are the guest, not the parent. No. 3 rule is to be prepared for that first question your grands are going to ask: "What did you bring me?" This appears to be a requirement for entry, like a visitation tax or something.

When visiting long-distance grands, there is probably a special event involved, and a holiday atmosphere, which makes the visit more exciting, more intense, and possibly exhausting. Be realistic. Is there enough room and privacy for you to stay comfortably in the family home or do you need to arrange nearby accommodations? This is what credit cards are for. If the family home is your only or best option, don't expect a private bathroom and control of the TV remote to watch an *NCIS* marathon. Also, the kitchen can be a sticky wicket. Some young folk are territorial, and if they say, "Thanks, but no thanks" to your offer to help, take them at their word. Nana and PopPop taking the children off their hands for a while might be more helpful, and that is what you came for anyway.

No matter who is doing the leaving, count on *everyone* being sad when it is time to go. It is best to keep the children informed when that departure date will be so they are prepared. Schedule your next visit together so there is something to look forward to. When it is time to really go, just go. Don't linger. Turn and go.

How do you survive losing contact with your grandchildren?

I want to address this because no matter the situation that brought you to this place, you are still a *grandparent*. No matter the situation, sorting out what you are feeling and developing a plan on how to deal with these feelings can be vital for your mental and physical health. According to an article written by Susan Adcox, author and grandmother of seven, you will feel grief as long as the separation exists. You may feel shock, and then anger. You must realize that anger is your worst enemy, and it may cause you to do something to worsen the separation. You *must* talk about this anger with a friend, a counselor, a pastor or religious leader, or a support group. I have known grandparents who feel they have been denied contact through no fault of their own and are confused and frustrated. Susan Adcox states that there are two possibilities. Either you are guilty of an error in judgment, and the parents are rightfully concerned, or the punishment the parents are handing out (separating grandparent and grandchild) does not fit the "crime."[9] It is up to you work through this.

- Honestly evaluate what led to the separation. Is this about unwelcome input you gave? Abuse? A family disagreement? Mental health? Parental divorce/custody rights? Misuse of power? Purposeful, willful ignorance of parental wishes? A court case? Are the parents in a new relationship you don't/can't/won't approve of? I have seen all of these. Are you a *victim* or a *cause*?

- If it *was* your fault, *apologize, apologize, apologize.* Do whatever it takes to restore relations with your grandchildren.

- If you still believe it was *not* your fault, apologize anyway. Do whatever it takes to restore relations with your grandchildren.

- If communication has been totally shut down, try to communicate through a *trusted* third party.

If you have tried and tried to work out the conflict with the parents and nothing has worked, then you have to move past the pain.

---

9   Adcox, Susan. "How to Cope with Losing Contact with Grandchildren." Verywell Health. Dotdash, December 1, 2018. https://www.verywellfamily.com/cope-with-losing-contact-with-grandchildren-1695992.

- Acknowledge that you have been betrayed by or you have betrayed close family members.
- Turn your pain over to your Higher Power. Prayer can heal a broken heart.
- Decide not to allow the sadness, fear, and worry rob you of joy and steal your life. No one will come to your Pity Party. Say daily, "I choose JOY!"
- Listen to "Let It Go!" from *Frozen* or "Bridge Over Troubles Waters" by Simon & Garfunkel. Music is cathartic. So are yoga and meditation.
- Join a Facebook group of other estranged grandparents. You are not alone.
- Volunteer for activities with children that will make a difference in their lives. Fill that hole in your heart. Or volunteer with causes that are important to you. This can be uplifting.

If in your heart you know it is *not* your fault, you may just have to accept the situation, but don't *ever* stop trying to repair the separation. *Do* investigate your legal rights of visitation in your state and join organizations that advocate for grandparents' rights. You must keep focused on what is best for you and especially your grandchildren.

Here comes the "hard to hear" talk: sometimes grandparents make poor choices. Sometimes grandparents have participated in improper, illegal, or immoral activities or allowed people into their inner circle who have participated in improper, illegal, or immoral activities. Sometimes grandparents are rightly denied visitation and/or communication by the parents. Sometimes the courts have forbidden the grandparents' contact with the grands. *Apologizing will not fix this.*

Still, there is always HOPE. If you are allowed by the courts, continue sending cards and letters to your grandchildren. Maybe, just maybe, *they* will walk to the mailbox the day your "love stuff" arrives. If you are not allowed, still write those cards and letters but put them in a box. Create a memory book for your grands of your life and your feelings, or even a scrapbook of their accomplishments from the newspaper—Honor Roll, sporting events, or graduation announcements. When that day comes when your grands are old enough to make their own decisions or— Hallelujah!—their parents open the lines of communication again they will know they were loved—*always*.

* * *

Long-distance grandparenting stretches your heartstrings and leaves you yearning for those real snuggles, hugs, and kisses. Keep your passport current, use your frequent flyer miles, pack some melatonin for jet lag, and get on that plane ... or train ... or bus!

"EVEN WHEN MY GRANDCHILDREN
ARE NOT IN MY ARMS, OR ON MY LAP, OR
IN MY HOME, THEY ARE IN MY HEART AND
THERE THEY WILL STAY FOREVER."

–CATHE DEROCHE

CHAPTER 10

The Second Time Around

GRANDPARENTING 24/7

Nearly three million grandparents and great-grandparents in the United States have legal custody and are raising their grandchildren because the biological parents are unable to do so. In addition, there are kinship caregivers—aunts, uncles, godparents and others—raising relatives' children, as well. And the numbers are growing. According to PBS *NewsHour*, the number is up 7 percent since 2009. Census figures show approximately one-fifth of grandparents who are raising their grandchildren have incomes that fall below the poverty line. And about a quarter of grandparents raising grandchildren have a disability.[10]

---

10   Cancino, Alejandra. "More Grandparents Raising Their Grandchildren." PBS. Public Broadcasting Service, February 16, 2016. https://www.pbs.org/news-hour/nation/more-grandparents-raising-their-grandchildren.

Grandparents become guardians for many reasons, and none of those reasons are pretty. Substance abuse/addiction/opiate epidemic (No. 1), poverty, termination of parental rights, incarceration, mental illness, death of a parent, and extended military deployment all contribute to this new familial unit of grandfamilies.

If this sounds like you, I guarantee being forced to cut into your own retirement time or benefits was not part of your Bucket List. Deferring your dreams to prioritize the dreams of your grandchildren became the new reality. Instead of saving for retirement, you are saving for college on a budget that is likely already stretched. You do what you gotta do. Some states have created kinship navigators to boost assistance to kinship families. Do your research.

I had quite a few of these Momma Nanas with grands who attended my centers. One said it was like starting all over again, but with no energy. They looked exhausted at the end of a long work day, picking up their little ones. But they did it with smiles on their faces and love in their hearts, and they would say, "I can do this. I *have* to do this. These are my babies." These grandparents are *my* heroes.

Caring for your grands 24/7, however, can also enrich your life, and give you something new to live for. It can keep you young. You will learn to text!

Even when there is a full rendition of the Broadway show *STOMP!* going on in your living room (now official playroom), or you feel like you have spent the last twenty-four hours manning phones at a Jerry Lewis Telethon. You are offering a safe, warm, loving environment. In return, your frazzled nerves and staggering responsibilities are rewarded when a grand grabs your hand before crossing the street; they know you will keep them safe. Or they bring you dandelions from the yard with sparkles in their eyes and say, "You are my sweetheart." Or they present you with a plaster-mold handprint on Mother's/Father's Day. You are their world. Their center. You are what keeps them whole.

So, how do *you* keep it together? How do *you* stay whole? Taking care of your grands is important but so is taking care of yourself. Self-care is not *selfish*. I am certain the physical, emotional, and financial demands are overwhelming. You may often feel that you cannot take another step, or that you cannot take the time for yourself because you constantly need to be present for your grandchild. However, like an athlete, you *must* take time to refuel and recharge. You need "me time." Maybe a friend or neighbor could watch the children while you take a walk, soak in a bath, or read a book. Just fifteen minutes works wonders. Give yourself permission to feel sad on some days and just have yourself a good cry—after the grands are asleep.

Eat nutritious meals. Get adequate sleep and try not to stress over the piles of laundry on the floor. Assign chores!

Recognize how special you are. If you have scooped your grands up before foster care could step in, then you have the strength and fortitude to do this. You have the commitment to keep the family together. You have the wisdom of experience. You have the *love*. I know you thought you would pick and choose when you were going to spend special times with your grands: an occasional movie; a walk in the park; a week at Disney or the beach; the Nutcracker ballet; dance recitals; soccer games; graduations.

But now you are back to homework, meals, schedules, and play dates. You have moved from luxury to necessity. Resentment and fear are normal reactions, and this doesn't mean you don't love your grands, it means you are normal. Most of our Momma Nanas experienced real anger toward their own kids for walking away and taking the grandparents' independence with them. Or they experienced deep sadness and mourning over the death of their own child. Or they experienced worry for their own child who was one of the 44 million American adults with a mental illness, and frustration with a system through which their own child couldn't find help. These frustrations mean you are normal. But not one of our Momma Nanas ever said they would have it any other way.

Just as you are adjusting to this major life change, your grand is also. Behavior changes are to be expected, and withdrawal or aggression are common. Not only are your grands dealing with a loss of a parent(s), but probably their home turf, as well.

Don't forget to notify the schools about the change in your family status. Too many times, we found out six months later and the changes in the child's behavioral patterns were set. Teachers, counselors, principals, directors, and school nurses are all there to help. This is not life's most embarrassing moment. This happens every day. Ask for help!

Tips from our Momma Nanas:

Stick to a routine and establish house rules (and enforce them!). For real, children want rules and routines. They want to know what is going to happen next. Saying, "In ten minutes we will be …"; "You have two minutes before we …" makes life so much easier. Activity calendars and chore charts will make everyone's day better. You might as well throw in a potty chart, because regression is sure to happen.

Make the grands feel welcome and at home, and involve them in building their new "nest," their new turf. According to our Momma Nanas, this was the best idea ever. An action hero bedspread or a unicorn poster on the wall establishes their space. A beanbag chair or a tee-pee in the corner gives them an "I need to get away from it all" place. Lucky for you, if you still have that tree house in your back yard. Children get overstimulated easily, so your goal should be to reduce clutter, induce calm. Young children thrive in brightly-colored environments, but I learned through teaching that ORANGE is a wildcard. It brings on irritability. My own boys had a very orange "Dukes of Hazzard" bedroom. Hmmm. That explains a lot.

According to a 2004 study by Naz Kaya and Helen H. Epps titled, "Relationship Between Color and Emotion," GREEN is associated with relaxation, calmness, happiness, peace, and hope. YELLOW is lively and energetic, eliciting positive emotions associated with the sun and summertime. GRAY is associated with negative emotions, including sadness, depression, boredom, anger, loneliness, and fear. Don't pick gray! PINK and BLUE will always be the gold standard for children's room colors. PURPLE is the "runner-up" for girls. Purple can slow down the hectic pace. Older children need calming blues, greens, and neutral colors.[11]

---

11   Kaya, Naz, and Helen H. Epps. "Relationship Between Color and Emotion: A Study of College Students." College Student Journal, September 2004. https://www.questia.com/library/journal/1G1-123321897/relationship-between-color-and-emotion-a-study-of

Don't get overwhelmed! This is not the time to go all Martha Stewart. A few new accents should do it.

Communicate, communicate, communicate. Communicate with the child, with teachers, with coaches, with Sunday school teachers, with Boy/Girl Scout leaders, with Social Services. Communicate with anyone who touches their lives. If you have a Guardian ad Litem appointed by the court, respect their responsibility to protect your grand's best interests. Talk to them, ask advice, *listen*, and do what they say.

TMI. Too much information about what has happened to your grand's family unit can be confusing and frightening. But they do need to hear the story from *you*. Be selective according to what's appropriate for their ages, and certainly be truthful. Children have built-in lie detectors. Even if you are just trying to protect them, they will call you on it. And be careful about what you say when you think they are out of earshot. Children might not respond to you saying, "put on your shoes" ten times, but if you whisper their name from three rooms away, they'll come running. "What? What did you say about me?" Adult conversations need to stay adult and away from little ears.

Encourage parent visitation. Whether the court has set up a supervised visitation schedule on neutral territory, or you are managing it on your own, it is up to you to help your grand get past their fears, nervousness, and insecurities. I have witnessed children so excited to see their parents at our center for a promised Mother's Day Tea or visitation, and then be devastated when the parent(s) were no-shows. I have also witnessed children so withdrawn from the parents who *do* show because they think their parents deserted them or don't love them, and now there is no communication. What was saddest were the photos posted in the office of parents who were never, ever, nohow allowed in our building.

What was joyful, however, was when everything clicked! These grandparents knew how to make it all work. These were the grandparents who kept the parents in the child's life through cards, letters, or technology. These were the grandparents who didn't speak negatively about the parent(s) in front of the child or poison the child's little minds with their own disappointments. These were the grandparents who understood they had received a gift, one that may be re-gifted someday. Or the grandparents who were going through the formal adoption procedure to choose "open" adoption.

It is up to you to decide whether you embrace this new lifestyle, and live life to the fullest, and experience that Fountain of Youth again, or wallow in self-pity and play the "poor me" card. Just remember, no matter your situation, your grand should come first, and you are not alone.

* * *

The 115th Congress of the United States of America enacted the "Supporting Grandparents Raising Grandchildren Act" in 2018 that was signed by President Donald Trump. This new act will establish a Federal Advisory Council that is an important step in supporting Grandfamilies. AARP, Academy of Pediatrics, and Generations United supported this act and are also excellent resources for your questions and concerns.

"SOMETIMES OUR GRANDMAS AND GRANDPAS ARE LIKE GRAND-ANGELS."

–LEXIE SAIGE

CHAPTER 11

Your Inner Child

GOOD ENOUGH FOR US,
GOOD ENOUGH FOR THEM!

Our grands find the fact that we were once children to be a difficult concept. Passing down our own childhood experiences to the next generation is an important roadmap to who they are. Create a time tunnel to your past!

- Look at your wedding album, baby books, baby pictures, yearbooks
- Listen to vinyl records, on a record player, and do the Twist; the Swim; the Monkey; the Jerk
- Play marbles; jacks; pick-up sticks; dominoes
- Roller skate (observe this one!). Did you wear your key around your neck?
- Read *Dick and Jane, The Hardy Boys*, and *Nancy Drew* mysteries
- Tour your house and discuss items that came from *your* parents

- Open your jewelry box with the pop-it beads, charm bracelets, circle pins
- Watch a black-and-white TV movie (one grand asked her mom if she'd only seen in black-in-white when she was little, like in PopPop's movies)
- Play shadow/flashlight/freeze tag; Simon Says; Red Light; I Spy With My Little Eyes; Red Rover; Hopscotch; Kick the Can
- Lie on your back and stare at cloud shapes
- Ride a carousel
- Make old-fashioned ice cream sundaes with whipped cream and cherries
- Count how many different state license plates they can find (keep a list!)
- Ride bicycles with baseball cards clipped to the spokes with clothes pins
- Catch fireflies in a mason jar
- Play The Telephone Game and Who Stole the Cookie From the Cookie Jar?
- Swing in a hammock
- Build a toy car track
- Play croquet
- Make puppets out of socks
- Go strawberry-picking—take powdered sugar with you!
- Make paper dolls
- Run through the sprinkler
- Flip baseball cards

- Make s'mores
- Go to a drive-in movie
- Ride a bus
- Parallel park a tricycle
- Paint a fence with water
- Build a fort with Lincoln Logs—cowboys and indians optional!
- Have a pajama party
- Play dress up from your attic: find your crinolines, go-go boots, poodle skirts, hats
- Go to an antique or hot rod car show
- Play Chinese checkers; chess
- Go to a '50s diner, and play the juke box, order an ice cream soda with two straws
- Have your picture taken in a photo machine booth
- Have a hula hoop contest
- Sit at a drug store counter and order A&W Root Beer in an ice cold mug
- Jump rope (Double Dutch?) to "Cinderella Dressed in Yellow;" "Teddy Bear, Teddy Bear Turn Around;" "Mabel, Mabel Set the Table"
- Taste honeysuckle
- Skim rocks on a lake
- Eat Cracker Jacks, Mary Jane candies, chew Black Jack gum, wear Wax Lips
- Make a time capsule
- Shuck corn

- Play Monopoly; Ouija Board; Operation; Sorry!
- Have a talent show or write a play
- Drive through a car wash
- Watch hummingbirds at the bird feeder through "you know, those black bird goggles" AKA binoculars (according to another grand girl)
- Go on a hay ride
- Chase an ice cream truck
- **PLAY OUTSIDE!**

Make your own treasured moments!

CHAPTER 12

Your Turn!
Your Bucket List

Imagine my surprise when I was presenting one of my seminars on *This Was NOT on My Bucket List* and I asked, "What is on *your* Bucket List?" and all I got was a room full of blank stares. Whaaaat? Granted, "bucket list" is derived from the seventeenth century term "kick the bucket," so maybe that is something people just don't want to think about. But the 2007 film, *The Bucket List* with Morgan Freeman and Jack Nicholson, was a great representation of the joy of experiencing life before it is too late. If you haven't seen it, watch it.

I truly believe that balance in our lives is necessary, and creating your personal bucket list is healthy and adds excitement to your life and whatever your future holds. It is never too late to jump in with both feet! If you haven't done so already, write down all those goals, dreams, and aspirations you would like to accomplish in your lifetime. Take steps to achieving these milestones and check them off before you cross that finish line. Keep a journal filled with photos, brochures, ticket stubs, maps, postcards, and menus. Document dates, times, and who you were with. How were you feeling?

I challenge you to write down fifty adventures you would like to experience. If watching your grandchildren is at the top of your list, so be it! Your list doesn't have to be crazy, wild bungee jumping or an over-the-top expensive trip to Fiji. I learned how to hula dance with a YouTube video—and no one was watching! Be creative! Carve out that special time from your busy life for *you*.

At the end of the day, I want you to be able to say, "I loved my life and I lived it to the fullest."

MY Bucket List

1. _____

2. _____

3. _____

4. _____

5. _____

6. _____

7. _____

8. _____

9. _____

10. _____

11. _____

12. _____

13. _____

14. _____

15. _____

16. _____

17. _____

18. _____

MY Bucket List

19. _____

20. _____

21. _____

22. _____

23. _____

24. _____

25. _____

26. _____

27. _____

28. _____

29. _____

30. _____

31. _____

32. _____

33. _____

34. _____

35. _____

36. _____

MY Bucket List

37. _____

38. _____

39. _____

40. _____

41. _____

42. _____

43. _____

44. _____

45. _____

46. _____

47. _____

48. _____

49. _____

50. _____

Nana's Pearls

My grandmother wore pearls. My mother wore pearls. I wear pearls. My daughter wears pearls. What is the mystery of the pearl? It is really just an irritating, tiny grain of sand that cultivates luminous, miraculous, one of a kind beauty. I believe the pearls we wear remind us of each joy, each sorrow, each achievement, and each lost opportunity we experience in the circle of life. As grandparents, we are like those grains of sand, adding treasured relationships and fond memories to our little grand pearls as we help cultivate them in to luminous, miraculous, one-of-a-kind beauties. No two are alike in size, shape, color, or quality. No matter how far away we are, no matter how many turns life takes, we are the guardians of these precious pearls.

It is all about choices. I choose to be that irritating, tiny grain of sand. I choose to go to the kindergarten orientations, the soccer tournaments, the shooting sport tournaments, the Odyssey of the Mind competitions, the awards ceremonies, the art shows, the graduations, the First Communions, and the dance recitals. I choose to be present in the lives of my grandchildren. I choose Nana's pearls.

The Bucket List can wait ... for now.

Final Thoughts

I have a confession. I started this book with all intents and purposes to whine about lost opportunities to check adventures off my Bucket List. Instead, this trip down memory lane has made me appreciate even more the ten amazing gifts God has given to me and I am full of life's promises.

I have a confession. I thought I had to be a perfect Nana to share my experiences and to be considered an "authority" in order to write a grandparenting book. Instead, I have learned that we all have stories and experiences to share that might, just might, help others. I decided lack of perfectionism wasn't going to stop me from wondering, "what if?"

I have a confession. I questioned that maybe as a septuagenarian (that's right!) it was just too late. But a favorite Rose-ism of mine from *The Golden Girls* is "The older you get, the better you get ... unless you're a banana."

I have a confession. I have enjoyed writing this book more than I could ever imagine. I sincerely hope you have had some laughs and learned some tidbits along the way. I welcome your questions and comments. We are all in this together!

Acknowledgments

Many people encouraged me to write a book—a business book, for independent business owners trying to survive day to day. But those days for me are done. It never occurred to me that I might have the wisdom and experience to offer advice to other grandparents *until* my fellow yogis at the Ellen Fitzgerald Senior Center in Monroe, North Carolina, began asking me questions week after week. Knowing I had owned several child development centers for twenty-plus years and was a proud Nana of ten, apparently I was considered an expert on temper tantrums, time-outs, and terrible twos. After teaching my first class titled, "This Was NOT on My Bucket List," at the senior center, I was hooked on sharing my experiences. I had done a great deal of research for this class, so why not a book? Namaste, ladies.

The Gold Medal Grannie Award goes to my mom, Nina Louise, who taught me what being a grandmother really means. Her sweet smile, endearing spirit, personal sacrifices, and genuine love for my children was an inspiration to be the best mother and Nana that I could be. I wish I had learned how to make her Southern fried chicken and gravy. BEST EVER! The Gold Medal Ga Award goes to my mother-in-law, Dolores, who was the stay-at-home mother of seven and one of the smartest and most driven women I have ever known. If you didn't have a summer job, she got you one. If you hadn't sent in your law school applications, they appeared in a manila envelope in your mail—filled out. Grannie and Ga were so different, but so alike. They both believed in *family first*. Even when their great grands started arriving, they both kicked it into high gear and Katy bar the door! Nothing slowed them down. Nothing got them down. I swear there was a Wonder Woman suit under their housedresses.

The MacPac. The curse of having an entrepreneurial mindset means you drag your kilt-wearing clan along with you on your journey. Fortunately for me, the MacPac has been supportive in all of my business ventures and there for me when I headed down Crazy Lane. They always had my back: painting walls, waxing floors, shoveling wood chips, whatever. They are my life. I couldn't breathe without them. In case you missed who they are, check out my Dedication. Their shenanigans are woven throughout the pages of this book.

My Sunshine Station Child Development Center family—teachers, children, parents, and grandparents were my heart and soul for so many years and I will love them forever. They taught me how to be a better person, a better friend, and a better grandparent.

Alliance for Children, a partner in Smart Start and the North Carolina Partnership for Children, invested resources and educational tools into Sunshine Station Child Development Center that allowed me to provide our children, ages birth to five, with the skills needed to enter kindergarten healthy and ready to learn. They encouraged me to achieve a Five-Star Rated License and National Accreditation (NAEYC). They inspired me to always put best practices above profit. Children First!

I offer a special thank you to Jeff Conyers, President of the Dollywood Foundation for allowing me to include the Dolly Parton Imagination Library Book Gifting Program and the use of Dolly Parton's personal quotes.

A final acknowledgment of all of the bazillion grandparents out there who love without limits, and a hope only to cross the finish line with a "well done."

Works Cited

Adcox, Susan. "How to Cope with Losing Contact with Grandchildren." Verywell Health. Dotdash, December 1, 2018. https://www.verywellfamily.com/cope-with-losing-contact-with-grandchildren-1695992.

Cancino, Alejandra. "More Grandparents Raising Their Grandchildren." PBS. Public Broadcasting Service, February 16, 2016. https://www.pbs.org/newshour/nation/more-grandparents-raising-their-grandchildren.

Dobson, James. *The New Dare to Discipline.* Tindale Momentum, 1996.

Edmonds, Molly. "Are Teenage Brains Really Different from Adult Brains?" How Stuff Works. InfoSpace Holdings, LLC, August 26, 2008. https://science.howstuffworks.com/life/inside-the-mind/human-brain/teenage-brain1.htm.

"Henri J. Breault, MD." Canadian Hall of Fame. Accessed May 26, 2019. http://http://www.cdnmedhall.org/inductees/henribreault.

Kaya, Naz, and Helen H. Epps. "Relationship Between Color and Emotion: A Study of College Students." *College Student Journal,* September 2004.

Kleinschmit, Matt. "Generation Z Characteristics: 5 Infographics on the Gen Z Lifestyle." Vision Critical. Vision Critical Communications, Inc., October 7, 2019. https://www.visioncritical.com/blog/generation-z-infographics.

Lehman, James. "How to Give Kids Consequences That Work." Empowering Parents. Accessed March 20, 2019. https://www.empoweringparents.com/article/how-to-give-kids-consequences-that-work/.

Madigan, Sheri L, Anh L. Ly, and Christina L. Rash. "Prevalence of Multiple Forms of Sexting Behavior Among Youth: A Systematic Review and Meta-Analysis." JAMA Network, April 2018. https://jamanetwork.com/journals/jamapediatrics/fullarticle/2673719.

"Respect." In *Random House Webster's College Dictionary*, 1147. New York , NY: Random House, 1991.

NAVIGATING "OLD SCHOOL" GRANDPARENTING IN A "NEWFANGLED" WORLD

Visit www.SOSNavigations.com

For serious booking inquiries,
email SOSNavigations@aol.com

CPSIA information can be obtained
at www.ICGtesting.com
Printed in the USA
BVHW032259221119
564529BV00003B/372/P

9 781734 126297